DOMESTIC CHÍC

A FASHIONABLY FABULOUS GUIDE TO COOKING & ENTERTAINING BY THE SEASONS

**By Chef & Nutritionist
Kristin Sollenne**

Published by Waldorf Publishing
2140 Hall Johnson Road
#102-345
Grapevine, Texas 76051
www.WaldorfPublishing.com

Domestic Chíc
A Fashionably Fabulous Guide for Cooking & Entertaining

ISBN: 9781943092178
Library of Congress Control Number: 2015936404

Anirays Camino Photography. All Rights Reserved
Copyright © 2015

Printed in the United States of America

Foreword by Cedric Jones, New York City Restaurant Group

Kristin Sollenne knows how to entertain and she definitely knows the definition of fun.

A few years ago, we were at a friend's wedding reception and we decided to take to the dance floor to show them how it was done. We got into our groove and began to dip, turn and twirl like a couple of contestants on Dancing with the Stars!

The other guests just stepped back to give us room.

That is exactly the kind of energy and excitement that Kristin brings to everything she does, including her first book, Domestic Chíc: A Fashionably Fabulous Guide to Cooking & Entertaining by the Seasons.

When we were opening Vucciria in the NYC Theatre District, Kristin introduced her progressive approach to traditional cooking. She taught us that Italian food doesn't need to be weighed down with heavy starches and thick creams to be delicious and appetizing.

As a certified nutritionist, she has long had a passion for fresh, healthy alternatives and teaches the importance of farm to table. In fact, the name Vucciria was inspired by one of the many fresh, outdoor markets in Palermo, Italy! Her Southern California meets Southern Italian charm is youthful and refreshing. In my twenty years in the business, I have never seen someone so focused on a food philosophy. Actually, it is Kristin who taught New York City Restaurant Group what a food philosophy is!

When we transitioned Vucciria to the Bocca Di Bacco brand, I had the pleasure of watching her spread her wings and share her knowledge with the television viewing public. Suddenly, she was in high demand as a television guest and as a cooking contest judge. Kristin took to television like basil takes to tomatoes. She simply lights up the screen as a Hollywood beauty with a heart of gold and one of the sharpest minds in the business.

I am always amazed at her tireless energy and how much she is able to fit into one day. In addition to serving as the Executive Chef and Culinary Director of New York City Restaurant Group's three Bocca Di Bacco locations, she has co-founded a charitable organization called the H.O.P.E Foundation, which supports education in the visual, performing and culinary arts. Also, she is making her footprint in the fashion industry with the launch of her kitchen couture designer apron line, CELLINI.

She has become a popular food, culture and lifestyle guru. Therefore, I shouldn't be surprised that becoming a published author is next.

It seems to me that Kristin just loves to share. Perhaps that's something she has learned from her close knit family. In fact, although she has added her special touches, these recipes have been passed down from generation to generation. Domestic Chíc is not just another bland collection of recipes, like so many on the market, and it's not just a how to guide on giving the best party. In it, she shares the family stories behind her favorite dishes. It is warm and welcoming, like a home cooked meal.

When it comes to being the best you can be, in and out of the kitchen, Kristin Sollenne is going to show us how.

Just step back and give her room.

Cedric Jones
New York City Restaurant Group

I dedicate this book to my dad, mom, brother, and loving fiancé who have always encouraged me to soar to new heights. Thank you for believing in me. I'm forever grateful for your constant love and support.

Introduction 15

INTRODUCTION

I'm not exactly what you call a typical chef, heck, when most people meet me I normally get the deer in headlights look when they find out what I do. Nothing comes easy, that's for sure, but with a good head on your shoulders and an imaginative and determined mindset, anything is possible. Luckily, growing up in a supportive Italian-American family, I was taught that I could be anything I wanted to be. Ok, in reality, maybe my family was so supportive at times that I really thought I could be ANYTHING. Nothing like positive reinforcement. I laugh now, looking back on my childhood and all the careers I told my parents I wanted to have...without hesitation their answer was always, "Great idea, Kristin!"

Now make a plan to make it happen." I had a lot of plans growing up, but I'm so thankful for their encouraging nature and teaching me that it's the failures in life that make you stronger, and when you get knocked down, roll over and get back up on other side and try a new way. My brother and I kept our mom pretty busy between dance lessons, soccer practice, basketball games, cheerleading, and swim team. After a long day, the time I cherished the most was when we all sat down around the dinner table, talked about our days and aspirations for the week, and indulged in a beautifully prepared, well-balanced meal.

Sundays were always the best! Family and friends would gather in the kitchen, talking and laughing all while my dad made the family secret sauce. (Yes, I'm finally unleashing the famous Sollenne Sauce recipe) I, of course, loved helping out, and developed a passion for creating and imagining new dishes to make. As I grew older, my passion deepened and I love transforming the table-scape into themed gatherings for friends and family that coordinated with the menu of the evening. Everything from planning to prepping, organizing and executing, I enjoy all aspects (well, maybe not the cleanup, but it comes with the territory).

One of my jobs while in college was working for a luxury lifestyle event-planning company in Newport Beach, California. I've always been the type that, if I don't know how to do something, I'll work even harder to figure it out and perfect it. We traveled to various cities such as Los Angeles, Las Vegas, and Chicago, hosting the ultimate luxury lifestyle exhibition event from all industries. This is when I fell in love with events and creating a one-of-a-kind culinary experience. To know your audience (customer) and please them is essentially the key to the hospitality industry, and keeps them coming back for more.

I always thought growing up that I would have that one "Ah Ha" moment and suddenly everything would be figured out and I would know exactly what I wanted to do. For some this may happen, and that's great! For me, it was a series of events that eventually led me to where I am now.

I received a call the day after hosting a Valentine's Day event. The call was from my mom, and I could tell from the tone in her voice that something was wrong. Her words were "He's ok now, but your father had a heart attack last night." With a million things running through my head, I panicked and didn't know what to do. I heard "heart attack" and "He's ok." Talk about a wake-up call. Immediately I turned to cooking and preparing healthy, nutritious meals for his recovery. My dad is the ultimate lover of Italian food. I swear he would pour sauce over his eggs in the morning if he could. This experience is what shaped my culinary philosophy.

Being a certified nutritionist and passionate chef, I wanted to create satisfying, yet nutritious, meals for my dad. I made a routine of visiting the local farmers' markets and would select in-season produce to center the meals around. After I saw the impact I had on my parents' lives, I knew this was my calling – I finally had my "Ah Ha" moment. So, guess what I did? Moved to the biggest, most challenging city in the world to make my mark on the culinary world – NYC, I'm here! On October 18th, 2008, I arrived in Manhattan with two suitcases, not knowing anyone, and unemployed. Talk about overcoming obstacles...I made a deal with my dad, as I normally do, and told him to give me two weeks and I'll have everything figured out. Luckily for me he agreed to the deal. I'm sure you've heard people talk about the energy of New York City, and let me tell you they're not kidding. I would wake up every morning raring to go, motivated and determined to start working in the industry.

Thankfully I have tough skin, it's basically a necessity in this industry, especially starting out, being a woman and, oh yeah, not going to culinary school. Needless to say, there was a lot of rejection in the beginning, but that only made me more determined to prove to everyone that I could make it. Sometimes, when you least expect it, the miracle that you've been waiting for happens. One and half weeks after moving to New York, I was given the chance of a lifetime and was working hard to prove myself. Here's some advice – Say "Yes!" Be enthusiastic about any job or duty you're given. Employers want to know that you're a team player and dedicated to getting the job done right. Be on time. This is one of my biggest pet peeves. I'm always early.

Employers don't want to hear excuses. Account for traffic, delays, and the unexpected. Give yourself plenty of time to arrive on time or, in my case, at least 15 minutes early.

I've been with the New York City Restaurant Group since 2008, and now oversee the expanding Bocca Di Bacco chain. In March of 2012, I had my first television appearance on WCBS Morning News. So, nervous and excited! In 2013, I was named one of Zagat's Top 30 under 30 in NYC. This was a surreal time for me. I then started to appear on the Food Network, judging for their competition-based programming and was able to meet some of my idols like Bobby Flay, Giada DeLaurentis, and Michael Symon. A dream come true!

I've always had a strong entrepreneurial spirit and learned from one of my amazing restauranteur mentors that you have to take risks to succeed. Besides cooking, one of my other passions is fashion. The evolution of the apron has always intrigued me, probably because most of my childhood consisted of being in the kitchen staring at family and friends wearing these unflattering pieces of cloth as they prepared meals. I wanted to create a brand of kitchen couture designer aprons that were fashionable yet functional and brought a modern-day twist to an old-style classic. I was lucky enough to partner with an incredible designer, Durango Adams, who brought my vision to life. Throughout this book you'll see me wearing the aprons, and I hope it will inspire you to entertain with passion and flair.

Speaking about flair – I wanted to provide you with unique entertaining and décor tips, so I enlisted the help of my dear friend and event planner extraordinaire, Monica Kline-Kazas, founder of Sweet Life Events.

Cookbooks can sometimes be overwhelming to tackle. They have amazing recipes but are always sectioned into Appetizers, Soups & Salads, Entrées, and Desserts, and it can be puzzling to try to pair dishes together. I wanted to provide you with a quick and easy go-to guide for cooking and entertaining, which is why I've written this book to guide you through the seasons and have pre-planned themed menus to coincide with Holiday's and celebrations. You'll discover fresh new dishes and family traditions, along with décor ideas for various occasions. Let this book be your one stop shop when hosting and entertaining – always being Domestic Chíc in a CELLINI apron, of course.

Most importantly, keep it fun – no need to stress. Relax and enjoy the process. After all that's what cooking and entertaining is all about! Something my mom taught me when I'm feeling overwhelmed is to think of everything as a slice of pie, and take it piece by piece until it equals the whole. Keep this in mind as you approach each recipe. First, thoroughly read each recipe from start to finish. Prep and organize all your ingredients. I like to put them in order as they are called for in the directions. Now you're ready to start cooking.

Ciao!

Chapter 1

Winter Wonderland
December | January | February

It wasn't until I moved to New York that I truly appreciated a real snowy winter wonderland and experienced the changing of the seasons. Growing up in California, we always had festive holidays, but nothing's like a white Christmas in New York City. As a child, the smell of freshly baked cinnamon rolls would wake my brother and me up, and we would patiently (yeah, right) wait at the top of the stairs until my mom and dad were ready with the video camera and told us we could come and see what Santa brought us. To this day, I bake cinnamon rolls every Christmas morning to keep the tradition alive. Enjoy my cinnamon roll recipe to bring a new tradition to your family as well.

Winter Produce Guide

Acorn Squash
Belgian Endive
Brussels Sprouts
Buttercup Squash
Butternut Squash
Cauliflower
Collard Greens
Jicama
Kale
Sweet Potatoes
Winter Squash

Clementines
Dates
Grapefruit
Kiwi
Oranges
Passion Fruit
Pears
Pineapples
Pomegranate
Red Currants
Tangerines

Christmas Morning Cinnamon Rolls

Filling
1/3 cup butter, softened
1 cup brown sugar
3 teaspoons cinnamon
1/2 teaspoon grated nutmeg

Cream butter, brown sugar, and cinnamon together. Set aside.

Dough
2 1/4 cups flour
3 teaspoons baking powder
2 tablespoons sugar
1/2 teaspoon sea salt
1/2 cup unsalted butter
1 egg
2/3 cup whole organic milk

Directions
For the dough, combine flour, sugar, baking powder, and sea salt in food processor. Cut in butter until crumbly. Whisk egg and milk together. Add all at once to the dry ingredients and whirl briefly to combine.

Turn dough out onto a floured surface (marble is best) and roll or pat into a square. Mix all filling ingredients together and spread over the dough. Roll up like a jelly roll. Cut into 12 slices. Arrange rolls in a greased 9-inch square baking pan. Bake at 400 degrees for 20 to 25 minutes. Remove from pan.

Icing
1/2 cup powdered sugar
1 tablespoon hot water
1/2 tablespoon milk
Dash of vanilla extract

Directions
Combine all icing ingredients together to make a thin glaze. Drizzle over cooled rolls.

Easy Caramel Sticky Buns

Filling
16 caramels (melted with ½ tablespoon butter)
3/4 cup pecan halves, chopped
1 cup sugar
3 teaspoons ground cinnamon
2 tablespoons raisins
2 tablespoons butter

Dough
2 1/4 cups flour
3 teaspoons baking powder
2 tablespoons sugar
1/2 teaspoon sea salt
1/2 cup unsalted butter
1 egg
2/3 cup whole organic milk

Directions
Preheat oven to 400 degrees. In a saucepan, melt 1/2 tablespoon butter, to prevent the caramels from sticking to the pan. Place caramels into the pan and constantly stir until melted. Pour into well-greased 8-inch round cake pan and sprinkle with ½ cup of the pecans.

For the dough, combine flour, sugar, baking powder, and sea salt in food processor. Cut in butter until crumbly. Whisk egg and milk together. Add all at once to the dry ingredients and whirl briefly to combine.

Turn dough out onto a floured surface (marble is best) and roll or pat into a square. Mix remaining ¼ cup pecans, sugar, cinnamon, raisins and butter and sprinkle over dough. Roll up like a jellyroll and cut into 12 slices. Place cut-side down in prepared pan with the caramel mixture. (Sprinkle with any remaining sugar mixture)

Bake 20 - 25 minutes or until lightly browned. Immediately invert pan onto serving plate and remove pan. Spread any remaining caramel over buns.

Whimsical Winter

A magical fanciful feeling comes over me when I hear the word 'whimsical', and this menu is a beautiful combination of flavors, textures and aromas to bring the theme alive. Achieve this feel by selecting a monotone or colorless tone, like classic white or ivory. Play with textures, and incorporate a white sequined linen while using various white china patterns from classic to vintage to modern. The key is to not be afraid to mix and match. Stagger your stemware in different sizes. Pair with lace or linen napkins. To complete your whimsical look, add a lighting effect (easy and inexpensive to rent a gobo tree) to create a floating lighting effect of your space, with snowflakes or patterns.

Growing up one of my favorite things to eat was Arancini, Italian style rice balls. I've tweaked the traditional approach to infuse it with the tastes of winter. Welcome your guests with scrumptious risotto rice balls filled with roasted butternut squash, melted burrata and black truffle.

Menu

Lobster Bisque
Black truffle

Roasted Red Beet Salad
Herb crusted goat cheese, green beans, toasted walnuts, lemon vinaigrette

Pumpkin Gnocchi
Butter Sage

Branzino with Parsnip Puree
Ocean striped bass, parsnip puree

Lighter Panna Cotta
Mascerated berries, Vanilla Fresh Mint

Arancini
Butternut squash, black truffle, burrata with balsamic sauce

Lobster Bisque

Ingredients
2 pounds lobster meat, cut into small chunks
2 cups lobster stock
2 tablespoons extra virgin olive oil
2 tablespoons butter
1 tablespoon tomato paste
1 medium minced onion
1 bay leaf
1 large minced carrot
1 sprig fresh thyme
1 teaspoon chopped garlic clove
1/4 cup brandy
1 stalk minced celery
2 cups heavy cream
2 tablespoons flour
1/4 teaspoon paprika
1/2 cup dry sherry
Truffle oil (optional)
Sea salt & freshly ground pepper to taste

Directions
In a sauté pan, heat olive oil over medium heat and sauté garlic, onions, celery and carrots. Deglaze the pan with dry sherry and brandy. Transfer everything to a saucepan. Slowly sprinkle in flour and heat the mixture until hot and then slowly add the lobster stock, cream and butter until the soup thickens. Add the tomato paste, thyme, bay leaf and paprika. Bring to a boil then simmer for 25-30 minutes, stirring occasionally. Drizzle truffle oil on top before serving (optional)

Roasted Red Beet Salad

Ingredients
2 large beets, scrubbed and trimmed
1 pound string beans, ends trimmed
1/2 cup toasted walnuts
1 garlic clove, sliced
2 tablespoons scallions, sliced
2 tablespoons extra virgin olive oil

Herb-crusted goat cheese ingredients
4 ounces goat cheese (separated into 4 pieces)
2 tablespoons thyme leaves, chopped
2 tablespoons rosemary leaves, chopped
2 tablespoons Parmesan cheese
Sea salt & freshly ground pepper to taste

Directions
For the roasted beets: Preheat oven to 425 degrees. Wrap each beet in foil and roast them on a baking sheet until tender, about 45 minutes to one hour. Once tender, cool the beets in their foil packet for a few minutes, and then take off the skin. The beets need to still be a little warm to be able to remove the skins easily. Thinly slice the beets.

For the string beans: Blanch string beans in a large stock pot of well salted boiling water until bright green in color and tender crisp, about two minutes. Drain and immediately place in an ice bath. Heat a large pan with olive oil, garlic and scallions. Add the green beans and continue to sauté for three to five minutes.

For the herb-crusted goat cheese: Mix thyme and rosemary together in a medium bowl. Season with salt and pepper. Roll goat cheese in the seasoning to cover the outside. Cut cheese into four pieces and lay on a baking tray, sprinkle with Parmesan cheese and put in the broiler on high heat to create a golden Parmesan crust on the goat cheese segment.

To plate, place beet slices in the middle of the dish, then string beans on top and top with herb crusted goat cheese. Drizzle with a lemon vinaigrette and toasted walnuts. Serve warm and enjoy!

Pumpkin Gnocchi

Ingredients
11 ounces goat cheese
5 egg yolks
24 ounces whole milk ricotta cheese
1 1/2 cups all-purpose flour
1/2 grated nutmeg
1 tablespoon honey
1 1/2 pounds pumpkin
1 tablespoons butter
7 fresh sage leaves
1 tablespoon grated Parmesan cheese

Directions
In a food processor, mix together goat cheese and ricotta. Mix until smooth, about three minutes. Gradually add all-purpose flour into cheese mixture and mix well. Add egg yolks and continue to mix together until completely blended. Add nutmeg, honey and pumpkin into mixture and continue mixing together until evenly mixed in. Lightly flour a baking sheet and pour mixture onto the pan. Refrigerate for one hour or more to harden. Once hardened, scoop out pieces to form a small ball. You can use a fork to flatten and add lines on top if desired. Boil gnocchi for one minute then transfer to a plate with grated Parmesan cheese on bottom. Place gnocchi on top and then sprinkle remaining cheese on top.

For the sauce, heat butter in a sauté pan and add sage leaves. Cook until leaves are crispy, about 3-4 minutes. Once done, pour over gnocchi, serve, and enjoy!

Grilled Branzino with Parsnip Puree

Ingredients
4 large Branzino fillets (6 to 8 ounces each)
2 tablespoons extra virgin olive oil
1/2 lemon, squeezed
1 tablespoon chopped fresh flat-leaf Italian parsley
Sea salt & freshly ground pepper to taste

Parsnip Puree

Ingredients
1 pound parsnips , peeled and chopped into 1/2-inch-thick slices
2 tablespoons unsalted butter
1/4 cup extra virgin olive oil
½ cup Parmesan Cheese, grated
Sea salt & freshly ground pepper to taste

Directions
Rinse fillets with cool water, and pat dry with a paper towel. Lightly brush olive oil over the filets, sprinkle sea salt and pepper, and grill over high heat on each side for about three minutes or until cooked.

In a large pot, combine parsnips with cold water. Place over high heat, cover, and bring to a boil. Continue boiling until tender, about 30 to 45 minutes. Drain. Pureé hot parsnips, butter, and olive oil until smooth. Stir in Parmesan cheese season with sea salt and pepper.

To plate, spoon parsnip puree onto the center of a plate, and place the fillets skin side up. Garnish with finely chopped Italian parsley.

Lighter Panna Cotta with Macerated Fresh Berries and Mint

Ingredients
1 tablespoon powdered gelatin, unflavored
1 cup skim milk
2 (6 ounce) containers low fat plain yogurt (or Greek yogurt)
1 teaspoon agave nectar
1 vanilla bean
1 teaspoon honey

Berries
½ cup strawberries
½ cup blueberries
½ cup raspberries
½ orange, Freshly juiced
½ lemon, freshly juiced
2 tablespoons Grand Marnier
1 tablespoon fresh mint

Directions
Mix milk and gelatin in a small bowl, and lightly stir. In a saucepan, combine yogurt, agave nectar, honey, and vanilla beans. Bring to a boil over medium heat and gently whisk in the softened gelatin. Set the saucepan in an ice bath and continue to whisk until mixture is warm. Ladle the mixture into individual ramekins and refrigerate for at least four hours or overnight.

Serve with macerated berries. Mix berries with freshly squeezed orange juice, lemon juice, fresh mint and Grand Marnier. Refrigerate and let sit for at least 1 hour. Serve on top of Panna Cotta.

Arancini
Butternut squash, black truffle, burrata

Ingredients
2 cups Arborio Rice
1 cup water
1 cup chicken stock
1 cup white wine
2 tablespoons unsalted butter
1/8 teaspoon saffron
1 cup Parmesan cheese, freshly grated
2 cups butternut squash, (cut into ½ inch cubes)
1 teaspoon extra virgin olive oil
2 Burrata Balls (about 6 ounces each, cut into ½ inch cubes)
1/2 tablespoon black truffle, sliced
6 eggs
Flour
Panko bread crumbs
Sea salt & freshly ground pepper to taste

Directions
Cook Arborio rice in water, chicken stock, white wine and butter for 25-30 minutes until al dente. Mix in saffron and Parmesan cheese, and cool mixture. Refrigerate for at least 2 hours or until hardened.

To roast squash, toss cubes in 1 teaspoon olive oil and season to taste with sea salt and freshly ground black pepper. Preheat oven to 425 degrees and roast for 20-25 minutes. Until tender.

Once rice is cooled scoop out desired size rice balls, and form into a ball. Using your thumb form a thumbprint into the rice ball and place roasted butternut squash, black truffle and burrata cubes in the center. Re-form into an enclosed ball. Roll ball in flour, then eggs, then Panko bread crumbs. Lightly Fry in canola oil for three to five minutes, until golden brown. Take out and poke with a toothpick, then finish in the oven at 400 degrees for two to three minutes, until outside is nice and crispy. Pair with desired sauce, serve and enjoy.

New Year's Bash

A timeless evening, focusing around the concept of time. The best New Year's, for me, is entertaining at home with family and friends, cooking up a storm, and ringing in the New Year surrounded by lots of love, laughter and great Champagne, of course! Italians believe that if you wear a new pair of red underwear on New Year's Eve it will bring you good luck for the coming year. Buy it early! Surprisingly enough, it's hard to find red underwear before New Year's Eve. I don't consider myself superstitious but I always follow the red underwear and lentils tradition. Chin Chin!

To enhance the décor use simplistic centerpieces while incorporating wall art, place settings, and accent pieces of clocks, watches, timepieces and anything else time-related. It's chíc, classy and, well, timeless!

Menu

Lentils & Sausage Soup
Sausage, thyme, leeks

Endive Salad
Plum tomatoes, capers, celery, olive oil, red wine vinegar

Penne al Gorgonzola
Walnuts, peas

Cioppino
Lobster, mussels, clams, scallops, spicy tomato broth

Ultimate Cheesecake with Fresh Berries
Mascarpone, strawberries, lemon zest

Lentils & Sausage Soup

Ingredients
16 ounces lentils
1/4 cup extra virgin olive oil
1 1/2 large yellow onions, diced
2 medium leeks, white part only, diced
3 cloves garlic, minced
1 tablespoon dried thyme leaves
1 teaspoon ground cumin
1 teaspoon sea salt
1 1/2 teaspoons pepper
3 stalks celery, diced
3 carrots, diced
3 quarts chicken broth
1 (6 oz can) tomato paste
1 turkey kielbasa sausage, cut into small pieces
1 tablespoon red wine vinegar
1/2 cup freshly grated Parmesan cheese

Directions
Cover the lentils with boiling water and let stand for about 15 minutes. In a separate saucepan sauté the onions, leeks, garlic, thyme, cumin, and sausage in olive oil. Season with sea salt and pepper. Add the celery and carrots and sauté until they are tender. Add the chicken broth, tomato paste and lentils. Bring to a boil and then reduce heat to medium. Add red wine vinegar. Stir occasionally until the lentils are tender, about one hour. Sprinkle freshly grated Parmesan cheese on top before serving.

Endive Salad

I learned this simple and easy recipe from my Nonna, and I love how light and fresh it is. I hope you enjoy as much as I do.

Ingredients
4 Endive heads, sliced
2 plum tomatoes, chopped
1 tablespoon capers
1/2 cup hearts of palm, sliced
1/2 cup radish, sliced
2 celery stalks, chopped
Sea salt & freshly ground pepper to taste

Dressing

This is my go-to dressing – Simple, easy and tasty!

Dressing Ingredients
2 tablespoons red wine vinegar
2 tablespoons apple cider vinegar
1 teaspoon Dijon mustard
1/2 teaspoon extra virgin olive oil
Dash of dried oregano
Sea salt & freshly ground pepper to taste

Directions
Combine all ingredients in a large mixing bowl. Whisk all dressing ingredients together and drizzle over salad.

Penne al Gorgonzola

Ingredients
1 pound dried penne pasta (substitute whole-wheat if desired)
1 tablespoon extra virgin olive oil
1 medium shallot, chopped
2 garlic cloves, chopped
8 ounces Gorgonzola
1/2 cup chopped walnuts
1 cup frozen peas
1/4 cup vegetable stock
1/4 cup dry white wine
Grated Parmesan cheese
2 tablespoons fresh parsley, chopped
Sea salt & freshly ground pepper to taste

Directions
Toast the walnuts on a baking sheet at 350 degrees until golden brown, about seven to eight minutes. Set aside.

In a large skillet heat the olive oil, and sauté the garlic and shallots on medium heat. Add white wine and vegetable stock and let simmer for one to two minutes. Add peas and season with sea salt and pepper. Cook for five to seven minutes. Add Gorgonzola to medium-high heat and simmer for one to two minutes.

In a large pot, bring salted water to a boil and cook the penne pasta until al dente, about 10-12 minutes. Drain and reserve ½ cup of pasta water.

Add cooked pasta and walnuts (leave 1 tablespoon set aside) to the skillet. Cook for an additional two minutes, stirring constantly. If the consistency seems thick, add reserved pasta water, little by little. Sea salt and pepper to taste and sprinkle remaining chopped walnuts on top. Sprinkle grated Parmesan cheese and parsley on top.

Cioppino

Ingredients
1 pound manila clams, scrubbed
1 pound mussels, scrubbed, de-bearded
1 pound uncooked large shrimp, peeled and deveined
1 1/2 pounds halibut cut into 1 inch cubes
1 sweet onion, chopped
3 large shallots, chopped
1 large fennel bulb, sliced
4 garlic cloves, minced
2 tablespoons extra virgin olive oil
1 teaspoon red pepper flakes (add more for extra spice)
1/4 cup tomato paste
1 can (28-ounce) diced tomatoes in juice
1 cup dry white wine
5 cups fish stock
1 bay leaf

Directions
Heat olive oil in a large pot over medium heat. Add fennel, onion, shallots and sea salt. Sauté until the onion is translucent. Add garlic and red pepper flakes, and sauté for another one to two minutes. Add tomatoes with their juice, tomato paste, wine, fish stock and bay leaf. Bring to a simmer for 45 minutes. Add the shrimp and fish and continue on medium – low heat for another 10 minutes. Add the clams and mussels until they are completely open, stirring gently. Ladle and serve!

Cheesecake Paradise with Fresh Berries

Crust
1 1/2 cups graham cracker crumbs
2 tablespoons sugar
1/4 cup unsalted butter, melted

In a medium bowl, combine graham cracker crumbs and sugar. Add melted butter and stir to combine. Press crumb mixture into a 9-inch pie pan. Chill for 30 minutes.

Filling
2 (8 oz) packages cream cheese, softened (to cut calories substitute one package for low-fat cream cheese)
16 ounces Mascarpone, room temperature
1 cup sugar
3 large eggs
1/2 tablespoon lemon zest
1 1/2 teaspoons vanilla extract

Directions
Preheat oven to 325 degrees. In a large bowl, using an electric mixer at medium speed, beat cream cheese and Mascarpone for two minutes, then add in sugar. On low speed, beat in eggs, one at a time until just blended. Add lemon zest and vanilla. Beat until just blended. Pour into crust. Bake for 1 hour and 15 minutes. Remove cake from oven and cool before serving.

Topping
2 tablespoons sugar
1/2 cup fresh raspberry
1/2 cup fresh blueberries
1/2 lemon, juiced
1/2 orange, juiced

Combine all topping ingredients and let sit in refrigerate for 30 -45 minutes. Spoon over cheesecake. Serve and enjoy.

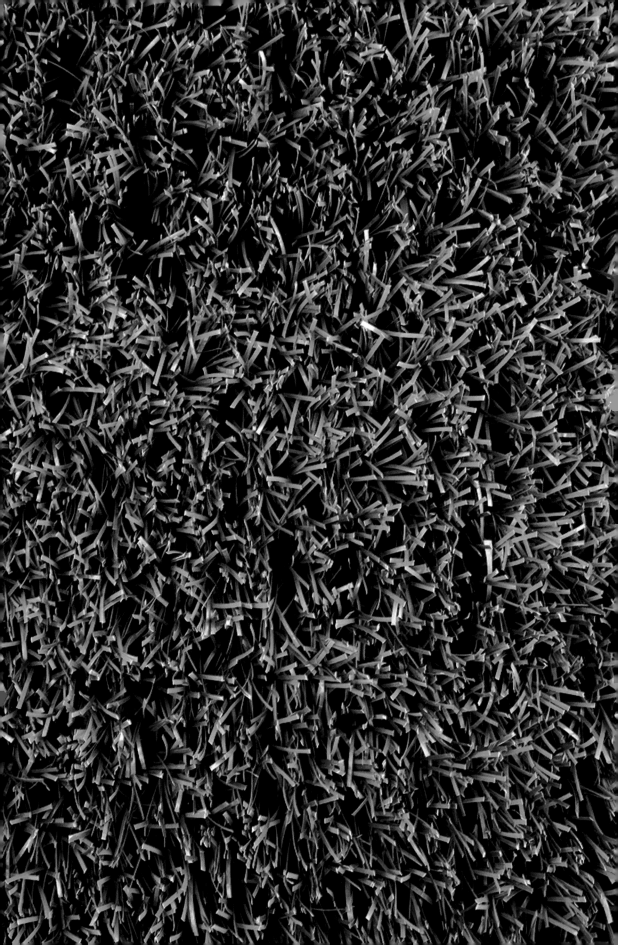

Football Mania

Why not turn your tables into your home turf? This menu is definitely a crowd-pleaser, showcasing an array of options that will please everyone's palate.

Easy and affordable, purchase Astroturf and wrap your tables with double-stick heavy duty tape. You can add to your buffet table by using colorful sports flags on toothpicks or straws to create a field. Suggest using only football-shaped plates, easily found at any party supply store. This creates a fun and festive kick-off!

Menu

Mixed Stuffed Peppers
Ground meat, rice, Parmesan, fresh tomato sauce

Hot Swiss and Almond Dip
Creamy Swiss and toasted almonds

Portobello Burgers
Mozzarella, rosemary

Cha Cha Chili
Ground meat, kidney beans, spicy broth

White Chocolate Chip Macadamia Nut Cookies
Vanilla, brown sugar

Mixed Stuffed Peppers

Ingredients
6 Medium sized Bell Peppers (assorted colors, red, yellow and green) (You can also use 16 mini bell peppers to achieve a finger food presentation)
3/4 pound lean ground turkey
3/4 pound lean ground beef
1 teaspoon dried oregano
1/2 teaspoon cumin
1/2 cup long-grain white (or brown) rice cooked
1 garlic clove, minced
1 small onion, grated
1 tablespoon extra virgin olive oil
2 tablespoons tomato paste
1 cup freshly grated Parmesan cheese

Directions
Preheat oven to 400 degrees. Heat 1 tablespoon extra virgin olive oil in a large nonstick skillet over medium heat. Sauté garlic and onions and cook until softened, about three to four minutes. Add the beef, turkey, oregano, and cumin. Cook through until no longer pink. Drain grease out. Stir in tomato paste. Season with sea salt and freshly ground pepper. Sprinkle in ½ cup grated Parmesan cheese.

Wash peppers and cut off tops. With a paring knife remove the seeds and core and any white pith connected to the flesh. Rinse inside of pepper and place in a baking pan. Cook peppers for twenty – twenty five minutes until edges have softened. Combine the meat filling and cooked rice. Fill the peppers, adding additional Parmesan cheese. Place back in oven and cook for twenty more minutes. Pour sauce* (Use Nonna Dina's Sauce Recipe pg.54.) over peppers and serve.

Nonna Dina's Sauce

This is the perfect recipe when you're short on time and need to pull a sauce together fast. Fresh, light, quick and easy!

Ingredients
2 tablespoons extra virgin olive oil
1 large onion, diced
2 garlic cloves, minced

Sauté above ingredients above for three to five minutes.

Add 1 large can tomato sauce (29 oz) (Nonna prefers Hunts)
Add 1 (6 oz) tomato paste and three cans of water. Use the tomato paste can to fill the water
1 tablespoon fresh basil, torn
1/8 teaspoon red pepper flakes (more if you like extra spice)

Sea salt & freshly ground pepper to taste

Directions
Add tomato sauce and paste to the pan. Season with sea salt, pepper and red pepper flakes. Add basil and simmer all ingredients together for 45 minutes.

Hot Swiss and Almond Dip

Ingredients
2 (8 oz) packages cream cheese, softened (to cut calories use low-fat)
1 1/2 cups shredded Swiss cheese (to cut calories used reduced fat)
3 tablespoons chopped green onion
1/4 teaspoon nutmeg
1/4 teaspoon freshly ground black pepper
1 cup sliced almonds, toasted

Directions
Mix all ingredients, leaving ½ cup toasted almonds aside. Blend well. Spread mixture into a 9-inch pan. Bake at 350 degrees for 15 minutes. Garnish with remaining ½ cup toasted almonds. Serve with toasted baguette.

Portobello Burgers

Ingredients
2 tablespoons extra virgin olive oil
2 tablespoons balsamic vinegar
2 sprigs fresh rosemary, stripped and chopped (about 2 tablespoons)
1 lemon, juiced
4 large Portobello mushroom caps
1/2 pound fresh smoked mozzarella, sliced
Sea salt & freshly ground pepper to taste

Directions
Whisk together olive oil, vinegar, rosemary and lemon. Coat mushroom caps and let marinate for 20 minutes. Grill mushrooms over medium - high heat starting with caps down, turning to caps up, about six minutes on each side. Pan-fry in a large nonstick skillet for the same amount of time. Season caps while they cook on each side with a little sea salt and pepper. Melt the smoked cheese over mushroom caps in the last one to two minutes.

Roasted Pepper Paste

Ingredients
14 oz roasted peppers, drained
1/2 tablespoon extra-virgin olive oil
2 tablespoons flat leaf parsley, chopped
1 large garlic clove, minced
4 large whole grain rolls, split (toasted optional)
Sea salt & freshly ground pepper to taste

Directions
To make the red pepper paste, combine the roasted red peppers, oil, parsley, garlic, sea salt and pepper in a food processor and pulse. To serve, place the grilled mushroom caps topped with melted cheese on the bun bottoms. Top with spinach and thinly sliced red onion. Spread the bun tops with roasted red pepper paste.

Cha Cha Chili

Ingredients
1 pound lean ground beef (or substitute ground turkey)
1 sweet onion, diced
1 garlic clove, minced
1/2 green pepper, chopped
16 ounces fire roasted diced tomatoes
1 (6 oz) can tomato paste + 1 can (6 oz) water
2 bay leaves
1 tablespoon chili powder
1/2 teaspoon cayenne pepper
1 teaspoon smoked paprika
1 teaspoon cumin
1 can red kidney beans
1 can pinto beans

Toppings
Sour cream (reduced fat)
Cilantro, chopped
Sharp Cheddar, grated
Chives

Directions
Heat olive oil in a large pot over medium heat, and sauté garlic and onions until translucent. Add meat and thoroughly cook through. Add green pepper and continue to cook until softened. Stir in tomatoes, tomato paste and remaining seasonings. Simmer for 1 ½ hours. Mix in kidney and pinto beans and juice. Continue to cook for another 30 minutes. Toppings are to be used as desired.

Arrange a do-it-yourself topping bar for guests to customize their own personal chili toppings.

White Chocolate Chip Macadamia Nut Cookies

Ingredients
2 1/2 cups flour
1 tablespoon baking soda
1/2 tablespoon sea salt
1 cup butter, softened
1 1/4 cups brown sugar
2 eggs
2 tablespoons vanilla extract
12 ounces white chocolate chips,
1 cup macadamia nuts, chopped

Directions
Combine flour, baking soda, sea salt and mix together well. In a separate bowl, cream together softened butter, brown sugar, eggs and vanilla. Mix wet ingredients and dry ingredients together. Gently mix in white chocolate chips and macadamia nuts. Scoop out cookie dough onto ungreased baking sheet and bake at 375 degrees for 10-12 minutes.

Lover's Delight

Nothing says "I love you" like a homemade meal. For this menu, it's all about the classical favorites and keeping it simple.

Décor Tip! K.I.S.S. Keep It Simple & Sultry. For an intimate party for two, cover the ceiling of your room of choice with heart-shaped red balloons filled with helium. Attach a ribbon to each balloon with a sexy message attached to the end of the ribbon for the evening entertainment. Set the tone of the room with reds and purples and light the room only with candlelight. Play with fabrics and textures to create an intimate setting. Love is a universal language, so not much is necessary to delight your lover!

Menu

Hot Crabmeat Spread
Jumbo lump crabmeat

Dad's Famous Caesar Salad
Homemade dressing, croutons

Squash Casserole
Yellow squash, zucchini

Grilled Lamb Chops
Balsamic and Grenadine reduction

Cannoli Siciliana
Ricotta, cinnamon, glazed cherries

Hot Crabmeat Spread

My parents lived in Maryland, which is where I was born, and is especially known for hard-shelled crabs. They would take their big boat Lady Patricia, named after my mom, and dock it to go to this special place to eat crabs. The crabs would be dumped in front of you and you would crush them with a mallet to get to the meat out. They were always hot, spicy and delicious. There is a famous restaurant in Ocean City, Maryland where they serve a crab dip that my mom absolutely loved. After asking the waitress several times from going there, she was able to piece the recipe together. She even has a special dish with a crab on it to serve it in, which makes it extra special.

Try this new and improved recipe!

Ingredients
2 (8 oz) packages cream cheese (to cut calories substitute one package for low-fat)
2 tablespoons milk
1 pound jumbo lump crabmeat
1 small onion, grated
1 teaspoon prepared horseradish
1/2 teaspoon extra hot horseradish
2/3 cup almonds, sliced
Sea salt & freshly ground pepper to taste

Directions
Soften cream cheese and beat with milk. Add onion, horseradish, sea salt and pepper. Mix well. Fold in crabmeat. Place in a shallow two-quart baking dish. Sprinkle with sliced almonds and bake at 375 degrees for 20-25 minutes, until browned and bubbly. Serve with sliced pumpernickel and/or crackers.

Dad's Famous Caesar Salad

I grew up with my dad making the best Caesar salad, and always loved watching him whisk the dressing together in his unfinished wooden bowl. He's used the same one for the past 25 years! If you don't have one, they can be a little pricey, but definitely worth the investment.

Ingredients
1/3 cup oil (canola or extra virgin olive oil)
2 garlic cloves, crushed
2 egg whites
1/4 cup grated Parmesan cheese
1 tablespoon anchovy paste
Dash of Worcestershire sauce
1 teaspoon ground mustard
1 fresh lemon squeezed
I large head romaine lettuce, cleaned and cut into 1 inch pieces.

Directions
Crush garlic in the bowl and then with a mallet add a tiny bit of oil and anchovy paste. Continue to rub together the garlic and anchovy paste then add remaining oil, constantly stirring (I like canola oil for the dressing). Whisk in the egg whites, grated Parmesan cheese, ground mustard, lemon juice and a dash of Worcestershire sauce. Season with sea salt and freshly ground black pepper. Add crisp romaine lettuce and toss to mix well. Add thin Parmesan slices on top for each serving.

Squash Casserole

Ingredients
3 cups yellow squash, diced
3 cups zucchini, diced
1 large yellow onion, chopped
2 tablespoons extra virgin olive oil
1/2 cup crème fraiche
2 garlic cloves, chopped
1 cup grated Cheddar cheese (reduced fat)
Sea salt & freshly ground pepper to taste

Directions
Preheat oven to 350 degrees. Sauté squash and zucchini in 1 tablespoon of olive oil, over medium-low heat, and cook until it has completely broken down; approximately 20-25 minutes. Line a colander with cheesecloth. Place the cooked squash and zucchini in the lined colander and squeeze excess moisture out. Set aside.

In a medium sized skillet, heat 1 tablespoon extra-virgin olive oil and sauté garlic and onion for two to three minutes. Remove from pan and lightly beat all remaining ingredients together. Pour mixture into a casserole dish and bake for 25 minutes, sprinkling additional cheese on top.

Grilled Lamb Chops with Balsamic and Grenadine Reduction

Ingredients
8 lamb chops
2 garlic cloves, minced
1 tablespoon fresh rosemary leaves, chopped
2 1/2 tablespoons extra virgin olive oil
1 cup balsamic vinegar
1/2 cup grenadine
Sea salt & freshly ground pepper to taste

Directions
Season both sides of the lamb chops with sea salt and pepper. Combine garlic, rosemary and olive oil into a paste. Rub the paste on both sides of the lamb chops and let them marinate for at least 45 minutes in the refrigerator. Remove from the refrigerator and let the lamb chops come to room temperature.

Heat the grill on high heat. Add the lamb chops and let sear for two minutes. Turn the chops over, and cook for another two to three minutes, depending on desired doneness.

On high heat over the stovetop, reduce the balsamic and grenadine mixture for 8-10 minutes, until consistency thickens.

Drizzle reduction over lamb chops before serving.

Cannoli Siciliana

Don't stress! Buy the shells and fill it with love.

Ingredients
12 shells (Can be purchased in any Italian bakery)

Filling
3 cups ricotta cheese
1/2 cup powdered sugar
1/4 cup cinnamon
1/2 tablespoon cocoa
1/2 teaspoon vanilla
3 tablespoons citron peel, chopped
3 tablespoons orange peel, chopped
6 glazed cherries, chopped

Directions
Mix ricotta thoroughly with sifted dry ingredients. Add vanilla and fruit peel. Mix and blend well. (A little grated pistachio may be added if desired.) Chill in refrigerator before filling shells. Decorate each end with a piece of glazed cherry and sprinkle shells with powdered sugar. Refrigerate until ready to serve.

My Favorite Winter Recipes –
from my family to yours

Eggplant Patties

Ingredients
2 large eggplants
2 lightly beaten eggs
1 cup freshly grated Parmesan cheese
8 large basil leaves, chopped fine
2 1/2 cup bread crumbs, plain
1 tablespoon minced garlic
1 teaspoon dried oregano
Vegetable oil for frying
Sea salt & freshly ground pepper to taste

Directions
Preheat oven to 375 degrees. Slice the eggplant in half lengthwise and place it in the oven for 30 minutes or until cooked through, but still firm. Let the eggplant cool and coarsely mash half the eggplant in a large bowl and chop the other half.

Mix the eggplant together then add the eggs, grated cheese, minced garlic, dried oregano, basil and pepper. Add ½ cup of breadcrumbs and stir until the eggplant is easy to handle and hold together. If the mixture is too moist, add 1/2 cup more breadcrumbs.

Form the eggplant mixture into flat cakes and dredge them in breadcrumbs. Heat vegetable oil in a large pan over moderate heat and add the eggplant patties. Allow each side to turn golden brown. Serve with lemon wedges and Nonna Dina's tomato sauce (pg.54).

My grandmother use to bake slices of eggplant and layer them on top of each other, with garlic, extra virgin olive oil, balsamic vinegar and grated Parmesan cheese. Slice one eggplant into ½ inch thick slices. Drizzle extra virgin olive oil on both sides and season with sea salt and freshly ground pepper. Bake at 400 degrees for 25 minutes. Slice two garlic cloves and mix ¼ cup extra virgin olive oil and ½ cup balsamic vinegar and ½ cup grated Parmesan cheese. Let baked eggplant marinate for at least 25 minutes and serve atop a toasted baguette slice. Simple, easy and delicious.

Lasagna Roll-Up

Ingredients
12 lasagna noodles
1 tablespoon extra-virgin olive oil
10 ounces broccoli, chopped
2 tablespoons minced green onions
1 (15 oz) container ricotta cheese
1/4 cup grated Parmesan Cheese
12 ounces fresh tomato sauce* (Use Nonna Dina's Sauce Recipe pg.54)
4 ounces shredded mozzarella
1 egg
Sea salt & freshly ground pepper to taste

Directions
Cook lasagna noodles in salted boiling water. In a 20-quart saucepan over medium heat, heat olive oil and sauté broccoli and green onions until tender, about five minutes. Stir frequently. Remove saucepan from heat and stir in ricotta cheese, Parmesan cheese, sea salt, pepper and egg.

Preheat oven to 375 degrees. Drain noodles and place in single layer on parchment paper. Evenly spread cheese mixture on each lasagna noodle and roll each noodle up in jelly roll fashion.

In a 12 x 8-inch baking dish pour ¾ fresh tomato sauce. Arrange noodles seam-side down in sauce. Top with remainder of the sauce and mozzarella cheese. Cover dish loosely with foil and bake for 30 minutes, or until hot and bubbly.

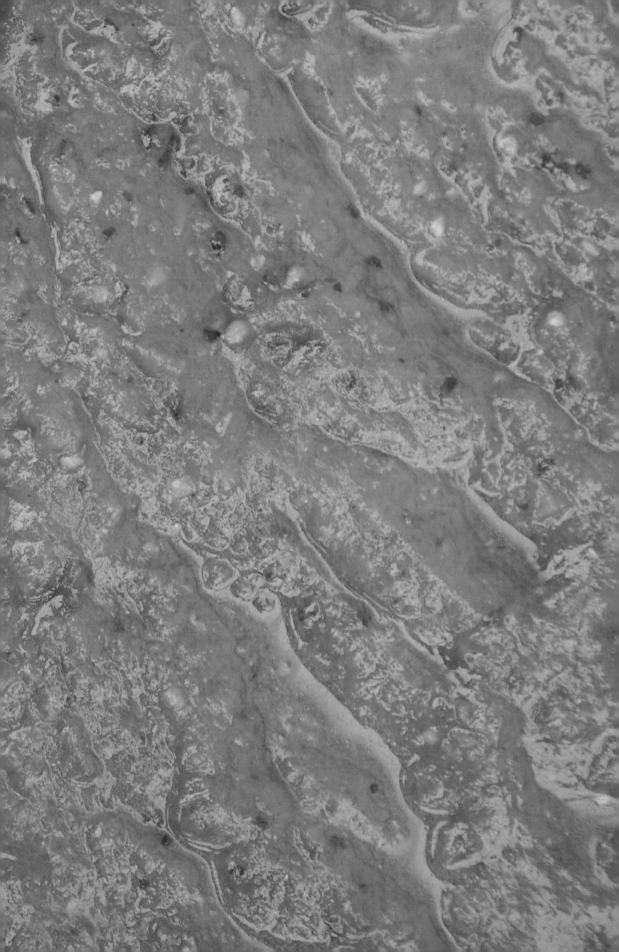

Sollenne Famous Sauce with Meatballs, Braciole and Italian Sausage

This is definitely a family-sized portion, so prepare to freeze some!

Ingredients
3 (29 oz) cans Italian plum tomatoes
2 medium yellow onions, chopped
5 fresh basil leaves, torn in half
3 garlic cloves, crushed
1 (16 oz) can tomato paste
4 mild Italian sausage links
2 tablespoons extra virgin olive oil

Directions
Heat extra-virgin olive oil and sauté garlic and onions. Brown sausage in the bottom of the pot. Crush tomatoes with hands and add to the pot. Add basil and simmer for 2 ½ hour – 3 hours.

Meatballs

Ingredients
1 pound veal
1 pound ground sirloin, lean
1 cup bread crumbs, Italian Seasoning
2 eggs
1/2 cup freshly grated Parmesan Cheese
1 garlic clove, minced
3 scallions, sliced
1 tablespoon chopped mint leaves
2 tablespoons fresh Italian flat leaf parsley, chopped
3 slices of bread soaked in milk for at least 30 minutes. Then squeezed to drain excess liquid
1 cup tomato sauce

Directions
Mix together veal and ground sirloin. Finely chop three scallions and mix with chopped mint leaves and parsley. Add this to the meat mixture along with eggs, garlic and cheese. Add drained bread slices and additional Italian seasoning breadcrumbs. Add tomato sauce until desired consistency.

Shape meatballs. You can either brown them in a small amount of oil or, for a healthier twist, place meatballs on a greased baking sheet, and heat oven to 350 degrees. Bake for four minutes on each side then put some in sauce to simmer.

Braciole

Ingredients
8 thinly-sliced flank steak pieces
1 cup bread crumbs
½ tablespoon extra virgin olive oil
1/2 cup grated Parmesan cheese
1/2 cup shredded provolone
2 tablespoons freshly chopped parsley
1 tablespoon crushed garlic
Sea salt & freshly ground pepper to taste

Directions
Sprinkle sea salt and pepper over the steak slices. Moisten bread crumbs in olive oil, and add Parmesan cheese, provolone cheese, garlic and parsley. Spread the mixture over the steak and roll the steak and tie steak with cooking string.

Brown on all sides in a small amount of olive oil and put in the sauce. Cook the sauce with the meatballs, sausage, and braciole on low to medium heat for about four hours. Serve with your favorite pasta.

Panettone

Ingredients
1 (.25 oz) package active dry yeast
1 cup warm water
1/4 cup sugar
2 eggs
1/2 cup nonfat plain yogurt
1 teaspoon vanilla extract
1 tablespoon grated lemon zest
1/4 teaspoon sea salt
4 cups unbleached all-purpose flour
1/4 cup dried currants
1/4 cup raisins
1 teaspoon unsalted butter, melted

Directions
In a medium bowl, combine yeast, water and sugar. Cover and let stand 10 minutes, or until foamy. Add eggs, yogurt, vanilla, lemon zest and sea salt. Mix well. Stir in currants and raisins and add flour ½ cup at a time until dough forms into a manageable ball. Turn out onto a lightly floured surface and knead for 5-10 minutes, adding flour as necessary, until dough is soft and pliable, but not sticky. Place dough in a large bowl, cover and let rise in a warm place until doubled. About an hour.

Preheat oven to 350 degrees and run butter around 8-inch cake pan. Punch down dough in bowl and place in prepared cake pan. Cover loosely (a dishtowel works well) and let rise 30 more minutes. (Loaf will rise above the pan sides.) Brush with melted butter and bake for 45 minutes or until loaf is golden brown and a toothpick inserted in the center comes out clean.

Chapter 2

Splendid Spring
March | April | May

The spring season is full of transformations. Flowers start to bud and bloom, and the sun's rays feel so nice on your skin after the winter. When produce is in season, that means there's an abundance of it and you can normally get it at a bargain. Some of my favorite items are artichokes, lychee and fennel. You'll always find a plate of sliced fennel on our dinner table to chew on when the meal is over to cleanse your palate. So refreshing!

Spring Produce Guide

Artichokes	Mustard Greens
Arugula	Pea Pods
Asparagus	Red Leaf Lettuce
Belgian Endive	Radicchio
Broccoli	Rhubarb
Butter (Bibb) Lettuce	Snow Peas
Cauliflower	Spinach
Chives	Spring Greens
Collard Greens	Sugar Snap Peas
Fennel	Vidalia Onions
Green Beans	Watercress
Jicama	
Apricots	Mango
Grapefruit	Oranges
Honeydew	Pineapples
Limes	Strawberries

Fresh Start

Longer days, fresh flowers and farmers' markets... surround yourself with the simplicity of the season. I bet one out of ten resolutions is to eat better, lose weight and start fresh. This is your ultimate go-to menu when you need to pull something together quick, easy and healthy. I start every morning with a glass of warm water, freshly squeezed lemon juice, cayenne pepper and a dash of honey. This is truly a fresh start to the day!

Incorporate fresh herbs, spices and fruits into your table-scapes by using fresh bunches of mint and basil in mason jars as décor. Fill apothecary jars with whole and sliced lemons and oranges... nothing freshens up a room better than aromatic fruits and herbs.

Menu

Salad Suite
Kale, cucumber, carrots, avocado, golden raisins

Carrot, Squash and Ginger Soup
Mint, basil oil

Skewered Shrimp with Jumbo Lima Beans
Fresh tomato sauce, basil

Salmon Filet with Sautéed Spinach
Butternut squash puree, spinach

Apple Brown Betsy
Cinnamon, brown sugar

Salad Suite

Ingredients
1 bunch kale
2 celery stalks, sliced
1/2 green apple, julienned
2 carrots, shredded
1/2 cup golden raisins

Avocado Vinaigrette

Quick, easy and tasty! Makes about 1 cup

Ingredients
1/2 avocado
1 tablespoon lime juice
1/2 tablespoon freshly squeezed lemon juice
1/2 minced garlic clove
1 tablespoon extra virgin olive oil
1 teaspoon Dijon mustard
1 tablespoon chopped tarragon
Sea salt & freshly ground pepper to taste

Directions
Mix all dressing ingredients together in a blender. Slice the kale by running your knife along the side of the stem. Then chop the leafy greens. Massage kale into dressing and then add celery, green apple, carrots and raisins.

Carrot, Squash and Ginger Soup

Ingredients
1 tablespoon canola oil
2 pounds butternut squash, peeled, seeded and cut into 1-inch pieces
3 medium sized carrots, peeled and chopped
1 large yellow onion, chopped
2 leeks, whites only, chopped
2 cloves garlic, diced
1/2 tablespoon thyme leaves, chopped
1/2 teaspoon nutmeg
1/2 tablespoon freshly grated ginger
3 cups vegetable stock (low sodium)
Sea salt & freshly ground pepper to taste

Mint, Basil Oil

Ingredients
1/2 cup packed mint leaves
1/2 cup packed basil leaves
1/2 cup extra virgin olive oil

Directions
In a large pot heat the oil and sauté the onion, and leeks and cook over medium heat for three to five minutes. Add the garlic, thyme, ginger and continue to cook for another three to five minutes. Add the chopped squash and carrots. Pour in the vegetable stock and bring to a boil. Simmer and cook for 45 minutes.

Puree the soup with a hand blender until smooth. For the mint/basil oil, puree the mint, basil and olive oil in a food processor until completely smooth. Drizzle on top of the soup before serving.

Skewered Shrimp with Jumbo Lima Beans

Ingredients
16 Jumbo Shrimp – peeled, cleaned and deveined
2 tablespoons extra virgin olive oil
2 garlic cloves, sliced
1 cup plum tomatoes, chopped
8 skewers

Lima Beans

Ingredients
1 pound jumbo lima beans
2 tablespoons extra virgin olive oil
1 cup carrots, diced
1 sweet onion, diced
1 cup celery, diced
1 garlic clove, sliced
1 cup dry white wine
2 cups plum tomatoes, chopped
1 teaspoon oregano
1/2 tablespoon parsley, chopped

Directions
Day before preparation – soak lima beans in water overnight. Peel, clean and devein shrimp and place two shrimp on each skewer and refrigerate until ready to use (optional). You can also clean the shrimp the day of.

In a large pan, heat olive oil, and sauté garlic. Add carrots, celery, onion, sea salt, pepper and sauté together for 8-10 minutes. Until cooked through. Add white wine, fresh tomatoes, oregano and chopped parsley. Continue to sauté for another five to seven minutes. Take skewers out of the refrigerator, and drizzle with olive oil, and season both sides with sea salt and pepper. Add skeweres and sauté for two min (or until color is pink) and then turn over. Add lima beans to the tomatoes and cook for 7-10 minutes until tender. Serve with lima beans on bottom and shrimp skewer on top. Garnish with fresh parsley.

Salmon Filet with Sautéed Spinach

Ingredients
4 large salmon fillets (6-8 ounces each)
1 teaspoon freshly ground black pepper
1 teaspoon sea salt
1 teaspoon lemon pepper
1 teaspoon dill weed
2 tablespoons extra virgin olive oil
1/2 lemon, juiced

Sautéed Spinach
Ingredients
1 1/2 pounds baby spinach leaves
2 tablespoons extra virgin olive oil
2 tablespoons chopped garlic

Directions
Rinse fillets with cool water, and pat dry with a paper towel. Lightly brush olive oil over the fillets. In a bowl, mix together sea salt, black pepper, lemon pepper and dill. Grill over medium heat on each side for about three to five minutes or until desired doneness.

Rinse the spinach in cold water and spin or pat dry. Heat the olive oil and sauté the garlic over medium heat, for about one minute. Add the spinach, sea salt, pepper and let sit for about two minutes. Stir occasionally with a wooden spoon, until all the spinach is wilted. Plate sautéed spinach and place salmon fillet on top.

Apple Brown Betty

Ingredients
11 medium sized apples
2 teaspoons cinnamon
1 1/2 cups flour
3/4 cup brown sugar
1/2 cup unsalted butter

Directions
Core and slice apples in eighths (peel if you prefer). Spread them over the bottom of a lightly greased 9 x 12-inch baking pan.

To make topping mix the flour, brown sugar and cinnamon together. Cut in the butter until crumbly. Set aside.

Syrup

Ingredients
2/3 cup brown sugar
1/4 cup hot water
Juice of 1/2 lemon

Mix brown sugar with hot water and lemon juice. Pour half of the syrup over the apples. Sprinkle the topping mixture evenly over the top. Pour the remaining syrup over the topping. Bake at 350 degrees for 60 minutes. Serve warm.

St. Paddy's Picnic

Leprechauns, shamrocks and the lucky four-leaf clover come to mind when you think of St. Patrick's Day, and it usually conjures up images of all things green. This is a fun themed menu, easy to prepare and a nice variety for everyone.

As a décor tip, embrace the pot of gold! Gold lends itself to some creative and trendy décor. Create your centerpieces using pots of gold with popcorn dipped in gold sugar. After all, isn't this really about finding the pot of gold at the end of the rainbow?

Menu

Tarragon-Spiced Deviled Eggs
Gorgonzola, tarragon

Paprika Corned Beef
Pickling spices, ginger

Stuffed Cabbage
Ground meat, rice, fresh tomato sauce

Arugula Pesto
Garlic, pine nuts, Parmesan

Irish Soda Bread
Raisins, pistachios

Tarragon-Spiced Deviled Eggs

Ingredients
4 hard-boiled eggs
3 tablespoons Gorgonzola cheese
2 tablespoons canola mayonnaise
1/2 teaspoon vinegar
1/4 teaspoon tarragon
Paprika
Sea salt & freshly ground pepper to taste

Directions
To achieve the perfect hard-boiled egg, begin with eggs at room temperature. Place eggs in a saucepan and cover with water by 1 inch. Bring water to a rolling boil. Remove pan from heat and cover. Allow eggs to sit for 15 minutes. Drain and rinse under cold water. Let eggs chill and then carefully peel under running cold water.

Split hard boiled eggs in half and scoop out the yolk. Place the yolks and Gorgonzola in a bowl and mix together. In a separate bowl, mix the mayonnaise, vinegar, tarragon, sea salt and pepper. Add just enough mayonnaise mixture to the yolk mixture to wet it. You want your mixture to be thick, not runny. Stuff the egg whites and sprinkle paprika on top.

Paprika Corned Beef

Ingredients
3 pounds corned beef brisket
2 quarts water
2 teaspoons mixed pickling spices
1 garlic clove
1 tablespoon extra-virgin olive oil
1 teaspoon soy sauce (low-sodium)
2 teaspoons paprika
1/4 teaspoon ground ginger
1 tablespoon brown sugar

Directions
Cover corned beef brisket with water. Add pickling spices and garlic clove. Cover tightly and simmer for 3 ½ hours, or until meat is tender. Remove meat from water and place meat fat-side up, on a rack in an open roasting pan. Combine olive oil, soy sauce, paprika, ginger, sugar and mix well. Brush mixture on corned beef. Bake at 350 degrees for 40 -45 minutes, or until topping is set. Let cool and slice against the grain to serve.

Stuffed Cabbage

Ingredients
1 large head cabbage
2 pounds ground beef (or substitute for ground turkey)
1 1/2 cups cooked rice (or substitute with brown rice, or quinoa)
1 teaspoon thyme, chopped
1 garlic clove, chopped
1 yellow onion, chopped
2 tablespoons extra virgin olive oil
2 cups tomato sauce* (Use Nonna Dina's Sauce Recipe pg.54.)
1 cup freshly grated Parmesan Cheese.

Directions
Heat olive oil and sauté garlic and onions for three to five minutes, until translucent. Add ground meat and cook until no longer pink, 7-8 minutes. Season meat with thyme, sea salt and pepper. Add cooked rice to meat mixture and 1 cup fresh tomato sauce.

Remove core from cabbage and parboil. Put a handful of meat mixture in the center of the cabbage leaf, wrap up and secure with toothpick. Put cabbage rolls in a large pan and cover with tomato sauce, and grate fresh Parmesan cheese on top. Cook at 350 degrees for 15-20 minutes. Serve warm and enjoy.

Arugula Pesto

Ingredients
4 cups packed fresh arugula
1 tablespoon minced garlic
1 cup extra virgin olive oil
2 tablespoon pine nuts
1 cup freshly grated Parmesan cheese
½ cup Pecorino cheese
1 pound penne rigate
Sea salt & freshly ground pepper to taste

Directions
Bring a large pot of water to a boil. Blanch arugula for 15 seconds and immediately transfer to an ice water bath. Squeeze the water out of the arugula with your hands until very dry. Roughly chop the arugula and put into a blender. Add the garlic, sea salt and pepper, olive oil and 2 tablespoons of the pine nuts. Blend for at least 30 seconds. Add the cheese and pulse to combine.

Bring a large pot of salted water to a boil, and cook pasta for 12-14 minutes, until al dente. Combine sauce and pasta and mix well. Before serving, add the remaining pine nuts on top. Mix ½ cup freshly grated Parmesan cheese and ½ cup freshly grated Pecorino together to sprinkle on top.

Irish Soda Bread

Ingredients
3 1/4 cups flour
1/3 cup plus 1 tablespoon sugar, divided
1 teaspoon calumet baking powder
1 teaspoon baking soda
1 teaspoon sea salt
1/2 cup butter
1 1/3 cups buttermilk
1/2 cup raisins
1/4 cup crushed pistachios

Directions
Preheat oven to 375 degrees. Mix flour, 1/3 cup of the sugar, baking powder, baking soda and sea salt in a large bowl. Cut in butter with pastry blender or two knives until mixture resembles coarse crumbs. Add buttermilk, raisins and pistachios. Mix until just moistened.

Place dough on a floured surface, knead 10 times and shape it in to a round loaf, 2 ½ inches thick. Place on greased baking sheet. Cut deep ½-inch "X" in top of dough. Sprinkle with remaining sugar. Bake for 45-50 minutes.

Mama's Brunch

Mothers deserve to have the red carpet rolled out! Growing up, we would always frame beautiful hand-written notes to our mom and place them around the house for her to find. Enhance the scene by using fragrant branches of lilacs and vintage china. Use floral-print napkins, silver teaspoons, tiered serving pieces, and a dash of pastel-colored sugar. Incorporate an eclectic mix of teacups that are fanciful, intimate and unique, just like the most special woman in our lives...Mama!

Menu

Smoked Salmon and Asparagus Frittata
Shallots, garlic

Crab Cakes
Crabmeat, shrimp, bell pepper

Italian Stuffed Artichoke
Garlic, olive oil, breadcrumbs, Parmesan

Curried Linguine Al' Vongole
Lemon grass, ginger

Raspberry Clafouti
Fresh raspberries, vanilla

Sgroppino
Prosecco, vodka, lemon sorbet

*Champagne Punch

Smoked Salmon and Asparagus Frittata

Ingredients
6 eggs
1 tablespoon of extra virgin olive oil
1 tablespoon shallots, minced
1/2 tablespoon garlic, minced
½ cup asparagus, thinly sliced
2 ounces smoked salmon
¼ cup whole milk

Directions
Preheat the oven to 350 degrees. Heat olive oil in an oven-safe skillet over medium heat. Sauté garlic and shallots until translucent. Add asparagus and the salmon. Cook and stir briefly to release the flavors. In a medium bowl, whisk together the eggs and slowly drizzle in ¼ cup whole milk. Pour eggs into the pan. Cook over medium heat without stirring, until the edges appear firm.

Place the skillet in the preheated oven, and bake for 10-12 minutes, or until nicely browned and puffed. Flip onto a serving plate, and cut into wedges to serve.

Crab Cakes

Ingredients
1 pound crabmeat
1 cup shrimp, chopped
½ tablespoon extra virgin olive oil
1 teaspoon garlic, minced
1 cup Panko bread crumbs
3 green onions, chopped
1/2 cup chopped bell pepper (red, yellow)
1 egg
1/4 cup mayonnaise
1 teaspoon Worcestershire sauce
1/2 lemon juiced
1/2 teaspoon Dijon mustard
1 tablespoon minced garlic
Dash cayenne pepper
Flour for dusting
4 tablespoons balsamic glaze.
Sea salt & freshly ground pepper to taste

Directions
In a large bowl mix together crabmeat, green onions, bell pepper, egg, mayonnaise. For the shrimp, heat ½ tablespoon extra virgin olive oil over medium heat and add 1 teaspoon minced garlic. Add shrimp and sauté two to three minutes until cooked. Add shrimp to crabmeat mixture.

In a separate bowl whisk together Worcestershire sauce, lemon juice, Dijon mustard a dash of cayenne pepper and 1 tablespoon minced garlic. Season with salt and pepper. Pour liquid into crabmeat mixture and thoroughly combine. Shape mixture into patties, and lightly dust with flour, then roll into Panko bread crumbs. These can be prepared earlier in the day and kept in the refrigerator. Heat canola oil in a large skillet over medium heat. Once oil is hot, place crab cakes in the oil and turn after four to five minutes or until golden brown. Warm balsamic glaze and drizzle over crab cakes. Serve warm.

Italian Stuffed Artichoke

Ingredients
6 large artichokes
6 tablespoons extra virgin olive oil
10 cups Italian seasoned bread crumbs
1 1/2 cups freshly grated Parmagiano-Reggiano
1 cup chopped green onions
½ cup chopped fresh Parsley leaves
10 garlic cloves, minced
2 tablespoons sea salt
1 tablespoon freshly ground black pepper
1/2 tablespoon cayenne pepper
1/2 cup extra virgin olive oil
6 lemon slices

Directions
In a large bowl add 6 tablespoons extra virgin olive oil, bread crumbs, Parmesan cheese, green onions, parsley, garlic, sea salt, pepper and cayenne pepper. Thoroughly combine.

Cut about ¾ inch off the tops of each artichoke. With your scissors, snip off the pointed ends of each artichoke leaf. Rub a lemon on the cut ends to prevent browning. Slice off the stem end of each artichoke so that they sit up straight. Spread the leaves of each artichoke as much as possible, and pack in a generous amount of bread stuffing. Stand them in a roasting pan that is just large enough to hold them in a single layer. Add water to a depth of 1½ inches.

Pour remaining olive oil over each artichoke, letting it seep in. Top each artichoke with a slice of lemon. Bring the water to a boil, cover, reduce heat and steam the artichokes approximately one hour or until the leaves pull off easily. Check the water level after about 25 minutes. Sprinkle grated Parmagiano Reggiano cheese over the top before serving.

Curried Linguine Al' Vongole

Ingredients
1/2 pound mussels, scrubbed and de-bearded
1/2 pound clams, cleaned
1 can coconut milk
2 1/2 tablespoons curry paste (yellow or green)
1 (2") piece lemon grass, minced
3 garlic cloves, minced
2 tablespoons ginger, minced
2 tablespoons fish sauce
1/2 cup white wine
1/2 cup onions, chopped
1 scallion, minced
2 tablespoons flat leaf parsley, chopped
1 pound Linguini

Directions
In a large pot over high heat, add curry paste and coconut milk. Dilute for one minute then add lemon grass, garlic, ginger, fish sauce, white wine, onions and scallions. Let sauce simmer for 25-30 minutes. Cook linguini until al dente. Add mussels and clams into the pot and cover until mussels & clams open. Add pasta and lightly stir in. Add scallions and parsley.

Raspberry Clafouti

Ingredients
2 pounds raspberries
3/4 cup all-purpose flour
3/4 cup sugar
2 eggs
8 ounces heavy cream
2 teaspoons vanilla extract
Powdered sugar

Directions
Preheat oven to 400 degrees. Butter and flour a 2-quart baking dish. Place fruit in the dish and set aside. In a medium bowl, combine the flour and sugar and blend well. Set aside. In a mixing bowl, combine the eggs, cream and vanilla. Whisk until well blended. Make a well in the center of the flour mixture. Whisk in the egg mixture to form a smooth batter. Let rest 15 -20 minutes. Pour the batter over the fruit and bake until the batter has just set and the surface has a light golden color. About 25- 30 minutes. Sprinkle with powdered sugar.

Sgroppino

Cleanse your palate with a delicious Sgroppino – in other words, an Italian smoothie. My favorite!

Ingredients
2 cups chilled Prosecco
4 tablespoons chilled vodka
2/3 cup lemon sorbet
2 tablespoons mango puree
1 tablespoon coffee grounds

Directions
In a blender, mix the sorbet and vodka. Drizzle the mango puree along the inside of each glass. Fill each glass halfway with the sorbet and vodka mixture and pour Prosecco to fill the glass. Sprinkle coffee grounds on top to cleanse your palate.

Champagne Punch

Every brunch need a great punch. Try this recipe for a different bubbly toast.

Ingredients
3 ounces grenadine
3 ounces Cointreau
2 ounces brandy
2 3/4 cups Champagne
Raspberries

Directions
Combine grenadine, Cointreau, brandy and Champagne over ice. Stir gently. Ladle punch into wide-mouthed stemmed glass. Garnish punch with raspberries. Makes four servings.

Fiesta! Fiesta!

Vibrancy is the key to a muy caliente fiesta! I've paired this menu together for the perfect culmination of sweet, spicy, salty and crunchy. Cover your space with oversized colorful papier-mâché florals, while accenting glass cylinders of various sizes filled with all types and colors of chili peppers. To ensure your guests can handle the spice, line an area with shot glasses of colorful shooters. Ole`!

Menu

Stuffed Dates wrapped in Pancetta
Bleu d'Avergne, parsley

White Corn Soup
Cilantro, cumin,

Shrimp Ceviche
Cilantro, lime, avocado

South of the Border Casserole
Ground beef, green pepper, jalapeno, rice

Cuban Flan
Toasted almonds

*Perfect Margarita | * Corona & Clamato

Stuffed Dates wrapped in Pancetta

Ingredients
24 Medjool dates
5 ounces Bleu d' Avergne cheese, cut and rolled into small balls
6 ounces pancetta (about 24 slices)
1 tablespoon, chopped parsley

Directions
Carefully slice the date down one side and remove the pit. Do not cut in half. The date should still be attached. Sprinkle in some chopped parsley to each date then fill with the Bleu d'Avergne cheese cube. Repeat this for all of the remaining dates. Wrap a pancetta slice around each date.

Place pancetta wrapped dates on a baking sheet, Preheat oven to 375 degrees and cook for 20 minutes, until the pancetta is crisp and the bottom of the dates are caramelized.

Transfer to a platter and serve warm. Enjoy!

White Corn Soup

Ingredients
2 boneless skinless chicken breasts
2 tablespoons extra virgin olive oil
1 1/2 tablespoon garlic, minced
2 tablespoons sweet onion, diced
1 1/2 teaspoon jalapeno pepper, minced
1 pound White Corn kernels
1 1/2 pounds, ripe plum tomatoes, chopped
1/3 cup Tomato Paste
2 1/2 teaspoon ground cumin
1 tablespoon sea salt
1/8 teaspoon ground White Pepper
1/2 teaspoon Chili Powder
1 1/2 cup water
1 quart chicken stock, low sodium
2 cup shredded cheddar cheese
1/2 cup chopped fresh cilantro
2 tablespoons crème friache

Directions
Over medium-high heat, heat olive oil and sauté garlic, onion and jalapeno; cook 1 to 2 minutes, until onion becomes translucent. Add half the corn along with all other ingredients (except cheddar cheese and cilantro), reserving other half of corn to be added at the end.

Bring the soup to an low, even boil. Simmer for 25 minutes. Remove soup from heat and let sit for 20 minutes. Remove chicken and set aside in a bowl.. Use a hand-held processor to blend soup to the consistency of a course puree. You can also process in batches in a blender. Using two forks, shred apart the chicken and return to the soup along with the reserved corn. Bring the soup to a boil, then reduce to a simmer for 25 minutes. Serve, with a dollop of crème friache, cilantro and cheddar cheese on top.

Shrimp Ceviche

Ingredients
20 large shrimp (cooked and cut into bite-size pieces)
2 cups plum tomatoes, chopped
1 cup sweet onion chopped
1/2 cup jalapeno chili, chopped
1/2 cup coarsely chopped fresh cilantro
1/3 cup fresh lime juice squeezed
1/4 teaspoon black pepper
1 tablespoon capers
1 cup celery stalks, chopped
1 large avocado, diced
2 teaspoons extra virgin olive oil
1 teaspoon sea salt

Directions
Combine all ingredients together and refrigerate for at least three hours. Serve with tortilla chips.

South of the Border Casserole

Ingredients
1 pound lean ground beef
3/4 cup diced onion
3/4 cup diced sweet green pepper
2 seeded, fresh jalapeno peppers, minced
1 (28 oz) can whole tomatoes
2 cups nonfat sour cream
1 tablespoon honey
1 tablespoon chili powder
1/2 teaspoon sea salt
8 ounces rice
1 cup shredded Cheddar
1 cup shredded mozzarella

Directions
Cook the ground beef over medium heat and drain the excess grease. Add the onions, green pepper and tomatoes, simmer until softened. Stir in the jalapeno peppers, sour cream, honey, chili powder and sea salt.

Add the rice. Stir, cover and gently simmer until the rice is tender, about 25 minutes. Stir every five minutes to keep the rice from sticking to the saucepan bottom. Transfer to a casserole dish and sprinkle cheddar and mozzarella cheese on top. Preheat oven to 350 degrees and cook for 10-12 minutes.

Cuban Flan

Ingredients
1/2 cup sugar
14 ounces condensed milk
13 ounces evaporated milk
8 ounce package cream cheese
3 eggs
1 teaspoon vanilla extract
1/2 cup sliced almonds, toasted

Directions
Caramelize sugar in saucepan over low heat. Pour into 9-inch cake pan, spreading evenly. In a food processor, combine milk, cream cheese, eggs and vanilla extract. Carefully pour into prepared cake pan. Place cake pan in a roasting pan and add about 1/2 an inch of water to the roasting pan. Bake at 350 degrees for 55-60 minutes. Cool, then refrigerate. Invert onto serving plate. Sprinkle with almonds.

Spring Specialties

I call it the four R's of Spring – Rebirth, Rejuvenation, Renewal and Regrowth. Don't you just feel great? Fresh fruit, herbs and seafood always excite me about spring. My mom always had great fresh snacks laid out in the kitchen that I would grab in between all my activities. This collection of springtime recipes is great for anytime of day. I hope you enjoy them as much as I do.

Panelle
Chickpea, Parmesean

Meatless Breakfast Taco
Egg, pepper, tomato

Spaghetti with Calms
Garlic, olive oil, parsley

Herb-Baked Cauliflower
Cilantro, lemon zest, dijon

Braided Easter Egg Bread
Flour, sugar

Seafood Risotto
Scallops, prawns, saffron

Panelle

I was introduced to this traditional Sicilian dish from relatives who were visiting one summer. Simply delicious and very easy! Sandwich this between a baguette and enjoy warm. I like to just eat it plain, too.

Ingredients
4 cups water
1/2 pound chickpea flour
1/3 cup extra virgin olive oil
1/2 cup grated Parmesan cheese
1 teaspoon sea salt
Canola oil for frying

Directions
Combine water, sea salt and chickpea flour and bring to a simmer stirring often, until mixture thickens. Add in olive oil and grated cheese. About 20-25 minutes. Spread out onto a pan about 1–1 ½-inch thick and let set in refrigerator until hardened. Cut 2" squares and fry in canola oil, three to four minutes each side, until golden brown.

Meatless Breakfast Taco

Tasty and healthy; you are going to love it! Very simple and fast to put together

Ingredients
8 corn tortillas
1 green bell pepper, diced
1 garlic clove, minced
1 medium tomato, diced
1/2 cup corn
1/2 red onion, diced
8 eggs
1 cup salsa
1 tablespoon extra-virgin olive oil
Mexican cheese blend, shredded
Sea salt & freshly ground pepper to taste

Directions
Plan on two eggs per person and beat eggs. Heat olive oil in a skillet and sauté garlic and onions. Add green bell pepper, corn and tomato and cook for an additional three to four minutes. Pour eggs in. Add enough cheese to cover the top of the eggs. Season with sea salt and pepper and scramble the eggs. Warm the tortillas. Put scrambled eggs in warm tortillas, and roll up. Drizzle salsa and extra cheese on top before serving.

Spaghetti with Clams

Ingredients
1 pound spaghetti
3 dozen little neck clams, cleaned
2 tablespoons extra virgin olive oil
3 garlic cloves, minced
1 large shallot, chopped
1/2 cup seafood stock
1/2 cup vegetable stock (low-sodium)
1/4 cup dry white wine
1 teaspoon red pepper flakes
2 tablespoons flat-leaf Italian parsley
1/2 cup grated Parmigiano-Reggiano cheese
Sea salt & freshly ground pepper to taste

Directions
Heat olive oil and sauté garlic and shallots. Add wine and let reduce for five to seven minutes. Add seafood and vegetable stock, sea salt, pepper and crush red pepper flakes with your palms before adding into the sauce. Simmer for 10-12 minutes until reduced by half. Add parsley and continue to simmer. Add clams and cover. Steam for three to five minutes until shells have opened. Gently stir. Discard any that did not fully open.

In a large pot of boiling salted water, cook spaghetti for 8 – 10 minutes. Transfer to sauté pan and finishing cooking for two to three minutes by adding ½ cup of pasta water.

Serve with additional parsley and Parmesan sprinkled on top.

Herb-Baked Cauliflower

Ingredients
1 head cauliflower, sliced in half, and then cut into 1" slices
1 tablespoon extra virgin olive oil
1/2 cup flat leaf parsley, chopped
2 tablespoons cilantro, chopped
1/2 teaspoon lemon zest
2 tablespoon Dijon mustard
1 tablespoon lemon juice

Directions
In a bowl, whisk together olive oil, parsley, cilantro, lemon zest and Dijon mustard. Coat each piece of cauliflower with the sauce and bake at 375 degrees for 15-20 minutes.

Italian Easter Egg Bread

This is a tradition in my family and we enjoy it every Easter. It's fun to get kids involved in the process and have them dye the eggs to decorate the bread with.

Ingredients
2 1/2 cups all-purpose flour, divided
1/4 cup sugar
1 teaspoon sea salt
1 (.25 oz) package active dry yeast
2/3 cup milk
2 tablespoons butter
2 eggs
5 whole eggs, dyed if desired (for decoration)

Directions
In a large bowl, combine 1 cup flour, sugar, sea salt and yeast. Stir well. Combine milk and butter in a small saucepan; heat until milk is warm and butter is softened. Gradually add the milk and butter to the flour mixture stirring constantly. Add two eggs and ½ cup flour. Beat well. Add the remaining flour, ½ cup at a time, stirring well after each addition. When the dough has pulled together, turn it out onto a lightly floured surface and knead until smooth and elastic, about eight minutes. Lightly oil a large bowl and place the dough in the bowl and turn to coat with oil. Cover with a damp cloth and let rise in a warm place until doubles in volume, about an hour.

Deflate the dough and turn it out onto a lightly floured surface. Divide the dough into two equal size rounds. Cover and let rest for 10 minutes. Roll each round into a long roll about 36 inches long and 1½ inches thick. Using the two long pieces of dough, form a loosely braided ring, leaving spaces for the five colored eggs. Connect the ends of the ring together and use your fingers to slide the eggs between the braids of dough. Preheat oven to 350 degrees. Place loaf on a parchment lined baking sheet and cover loosely with a damp towel. Place loaf in a warm place and let rise until doubles in bulk, about 45 minutes. Brush risen loaf with melted butter. Bake in preheated oven for 50 -55 minutes, or until golden.

Seafood Risotto

The citrus pairs nicely with the seafood and adds great flavor.

Ingredients
Juice of 1 orange
Juice of 1/2 grapefruit
3/4 pound small scallops
3/4 pound medium shrimp, peeled, deveined
8 large prawns
1/4 cup extra virgin olive oil
1/2 cup finely minced shallots
2 cups Arborio rice
2 cups vegetable stock
2 cups seafood stock
Large pinch of saffron threads
1/4 pound small shitake mushrooms, sliced
1 cup freshly grated Parmesan cheese
2 tablespoons chopped fresh flat leaf parsley

Directions
Marinate scallops in orange juice for 30 minutes. Marinate shrimp in grapefruit juice for 30 minutes. Heat 2 tablespoons extra-virgin olive oil and sauté shallots until tender, but not browned. Add rice and sauté until it turns opaque.

Add ½ cup boiling stock (equally divided between vegetable and seafood) and the saffron to the saucepan. Cook this over medium heat, stirring constantly, until all the liquid is absorbed. Add ½ cup more boiling stock, stirring constantly. Continue this until all stock is used and the rice is tender, but still a bit firm. The rice should be cooked and all the liquid absorbed in 20-25 minutes. Remove from heat and keep warm.

In a skillet, heat 1 tablespoon extra virgin olive oil and sauté the scallops and mushrooms (about three minutes), shrimp and prawns just until they turn pink. Stir fish into the risotto. Frequently stir.

Over low heat, stir the Parmesan cheese into the risotto. Season to taste with sea salt and pepper then add chopped parsley. Serve warm.

Chapter 3

Summer Sizzle
June | July | August

Growing up, this was my absolute favorite time of year! Finally out of school and on summer break. My favorite summers were spent in upstate New York, where my mom and dad grew up (sometimes referred to as the middle of nowhere). The first stop was always to The Caboose, the best hot dog stand around, serving white-hots with grilled onions and hot mustard. My Poppy (Mom's dad) had a cottage on the Erie Canal, with a boat and Jet Ski. In fact, this was where I learned how to water ski. But more importantly, this is where I began learning the art of the grill, and there's no better season for it than summer.

Summer Produce Guide

Arugula	Okra
Beets	Radishes
Broccoli	Red Leaf Lettuce
Butter (Bibb) Lettuce	Snow Peas
Cucumbers	Sugar Snap Peas
Eggplant	Summer Squash
Endive	Swiss Chard
Green Beans	Tomatoes
Hot Peppers	Zucchini

Apricots	Honeydew Melons
Asian Pears	Limes
Black Currants	Loganberries
Blackberries	Nectarines
Blueberries	Passion Fruit
Boysenberries	Peaches
Cantaloupe	Pineapples
Cherries	Plums
Elderberries	Raspberries
Figs	Strawberries
Grapes	Watermelon

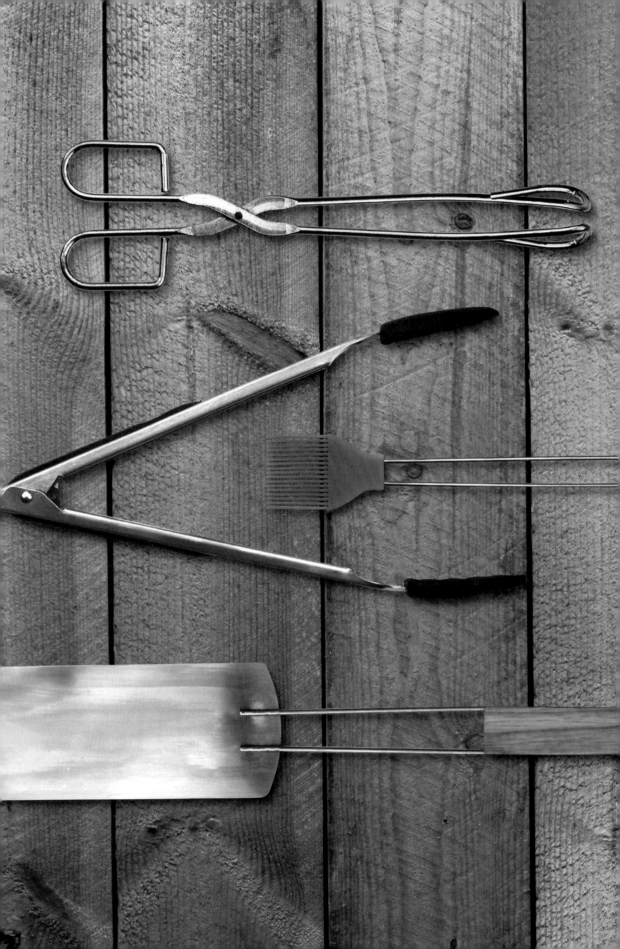

BBQ – Galore

Beach balls, bonfires and barbecuing...It's time to heat things up! Instead of roasting or baking, try to utilize the grill as much as possible with your meats, vegetables, fish, poultry and vegetables. Use colorful lanterns to illuminate your space, while having mini fire pits for guest to linger around. By incorporating the element of fire, it is sure to set the tone for a sizzling evening.

Menu

Roasted Vegetables
Zucchini, eggplant, bell pepper

Shrimp Scampi
Garlic and olive oil

Garlic Parmesan Olives
Basil, red pepper

Cucumber Bisque
Fresh mint

BBQ Chicken with Peter's famous BBQ Sauce
Organic chicken breasts

California Almond Fudge Pie
Amaretto

Roasted Vegetables

Ingredients
8 zucchinis, peeled and chopped
1 eggplant, peeled and diced
8 carrots, diced
16 cherry tomatoes, sliced in half
2 red onions, sliced
1 red bell pepper, sliced
1 yellow bell pepper, sliced
8 tablespoons extra-virgin olive oil
1 teaspoon dried rosemary
1 teaspoon dried thyme
2 bay leaves, crushed
1 teaspoon dried oregano
2 garlic cloves, minced
2 tablespoons grated lemon zest
1 lemon, juiced
1/2 cup low sodium vegetable broth
Sea salt & freshly ground pepper to taste

Directions
In a large bowl mix the zucchini, carrots, eggplant, tomatoes, onions and peppers with the oil, rosemary, thyme, bay leaves, oregano, garlic, lemon juice, lemon zest, sea salt and pepper. Cover and let sit for at least two hours.

Preheat oven to 400 degrees. Place all vegetables on a large roasting pan, and drizzle vegetable broth over vegetables. Roast uncovered for 20 minutes or until the tomatoes have split and the edges of some of the vegetables are starting to crisp. Remove from the oven and stir before returning to the oven for another 25 minutes.

Garlic Parmesan Olives

Ingredients
6 ounces black olives
6 ounces green olives
1 garlic clove, minced
1/2 teaspoon dried basil
1/2 teaspoon ground black pepper
1 tablespoon extra-virgin olive oil
3 tablespoons grated Parmesan cheese
1/4 teaspoon red pepper flakes for spice (Add additional if you like it hot!)

Directions
In a small bowl, combine, garlic, basil, black pepper, red pepper, olive oil and Parmesan cheese. Mix well. Stir in the olives until thoroughly coated .Marinate in refrigerator for at least one hour before serving.

Cucumber Bisque

Ingredients
1 onion, chopped
1 tablespoon flour
1 tablespoon extra virgin olive oil
4 cucumbers, seeded, peeled and chopped
12 ounces low-sodium vegetable broth
1 1/2 cups plain low-fat yogurt
1/4 cup dill weed
1/2 avocado, diced
1/2 tablespoon lemon juice
1/2 tablespoon lime juice
Sea salt & freshly ground pepper to taste

Directions
In a saucepan, heat olive oil and sauté onion, stirring occasionally for three to four minutes. Stir in flour, and add cucumbers. Add broth, and bring to a boil. Cover and simmer over low heat, about 30 minutes. Cool slightly and puree with a hand blender. Chill. Once cold, stir in yogurt with wire whisk. Add lemon juice, lime juice, sea salt, pepper and dill weed.

BBQ Chicken with Peter's famous BBQ Sauce

Ingredients
3 pounds boneless, skinless chicken breasts

Sauce Ingredients
1 1/2 cups cider vinegar
1 tablespoon garlic powder
1/2 tablespoon sea salt
1/2 tablespoon black pepper
1 tablespoon chili powder
1 cup granulated sugar
1 1/4 cups brown sugar
1/4 cup lemon juice
1/4 cup Worcestershire sauce
4 1/2 cups ketchup
3/4 cup molasses
1/2 cup extra virgin olive oil
1 tablespoon onion, minced

Directions
In a large saucepan, combine all sauce ingredients in order listed. Simmer over low heat for 45 minutes. Brush this sauce generously on chicken breasts.

Arrange chicken parts on the grill over medium heat. Continue to baste chicken with the sauce and grill chicken on 10 minutes per side, turning once. Drizzle additional sauce over chicken before serving.

California Almond Fudge Pie

Crust
2 cups flour
2/3 cup butter
3/4 cup almonds, coarsely chopped
1/4 cup brown sugar, firmly packed
1 tablespoon Amaretto
1/2 teaspoon almond extract

Filling
1/2 cup butter, softened
2/3 cup sugar
4 ounces unsweetened chocolate, melted
2 eggs
1 tablespoon Amaretto
1/2 teaspoon almond extract

Directions
For the crust, combine flour and butter in a medium bowl and mix until mixture is coarse and crumbly. Gently blend in almonds and sugar. Pour in Amaretto and almond extract over mixture and toss together adding more Amaretto or water as needed, to form dough into a ball. Press into bottom and sides of a 9-inch pie plate. There will be extra dough. Spread it on a small heat-proof dish, making it the same thickness as the crust. Bake at 375 degrees along with crust, until both are set and browned, about 10-15 minutes. Let cool.

For the filling, cream butter and gradually add sugar. Beat until mixture is light and fluffy. Stir in chocolate and add eggs one at a time, beating well after each addition. Stir in Amaretto and almond extract. Pour into prepared crust and spreading evenly.

Crumble the extra baked pie crust and sprinkle over filling. Chill well or overnight.
Great dish to make a day in advance!

All about the D-A-D

Knock one out of the park for your father this year with a protein-based, delicious menu. Here are some tips to help you with that: Your steak should be at room temperature before grilling. Make sure your grill is well heated before placing your meat on the rack. Let it sit and get a nice sear. Don't try to flip it too early; that's what will make it stick to the grate.

Instead of picking and sticking to one sports theme, why not plan the ultimate tailgate party to honor your MVP? Stanchion off your sections by using colorful sport pennant flags of your MVP's favorite team. Incorporate a table in each section so guests can roam from one tailgate to the next with ease. Use green Astroturf to create the tables, and use all types of balls as centerpieces and décor in each section. For example, in the basketball section, have a hoop available, and in the football section, incorporate a simplistic blow-up football kick off display. If you really want to create a tailgate feel, you can rent a bed of a truck from a prop house and use it to serve your meals while positioning it next to the BBQ. Dad will really feel like an all-star at this tailgate in his honor.

Menu

Stuffed Mushrooms
Oregano, bread crumbs, mozzarella and Romano

Lobster Salad with Cucumber and Avocado
Parsley, fresh lemon juice

Orecchiette with Sausage and Spinach
Sweet Italian sausage, garlic, olive oil

Grilled Angus Sirloin Steak
Barolo reduction

Pecan Pie
Toasted pecans

Stuffed Mushrooms

Ingredients
1/2 tablespoon garlic, chopped
1 tablespoon oregano
1 tablespoon basil, chopped
1 tablespoon parsley, chopped
2 tablespoons Pecorino Romano cheese, grated
2 tablespoons mozzarella cheese, shredded
1 cup Italian seasoned bread crumbs
24 mushrooms caps
2 tablespoons extra virgin olive oil
Sea salt & freshly ground pepper to taste

Directions
Clean mushrooms thoroughly. In a mixing bowl stir in the oregano, basil, parsley, mozarella, Pecorino, breadcrumbs, garlic and two tablespoons olive oil. Stuff each mushroom cap and place it on a baking sheet. Bake at 350 for 15-20 minutes until golden brown on top.

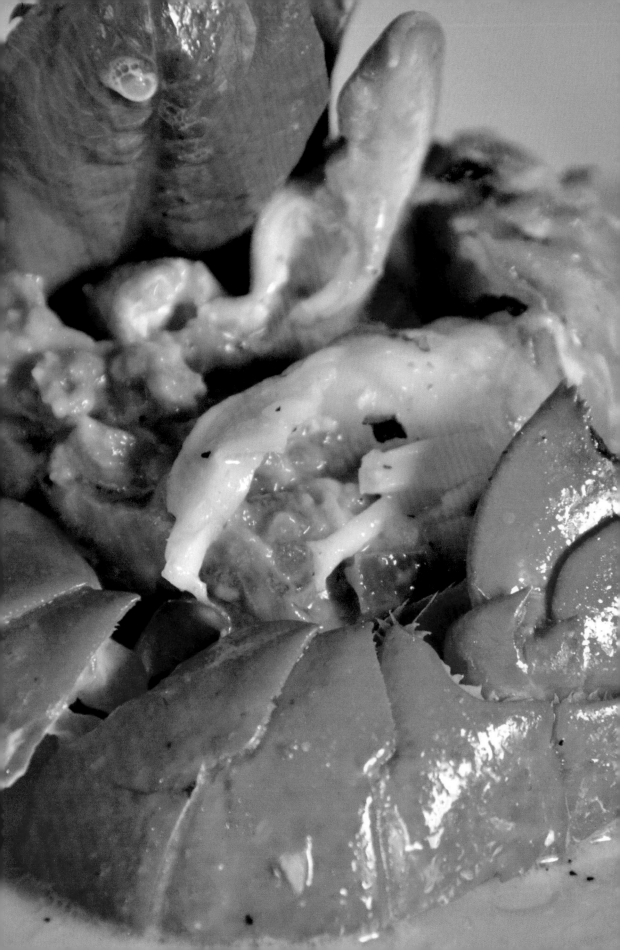

Lobster Salad with Cucumber and Avocado

Ingredients
2 Avocados sliced
1 cucumber, thinly sliced
2 (1 pound) lobsters
2 tablespoons balsamic glaze

Dressing Ingredients
2 tablespoons fresh lemon juice
1/4 cup extra virgin olive oil
1/2 tablespoon chopped parsley
Sea salt and freshly ground black pepper to taste

Directions
Boil lobster in a large pot for five-seven minutes. Remove the lobster from the boiling water and immediately plunge it into an ice cold water bath. Remove the lobster and twist off the tails removing the meat inside. Cut the shell in half and remove the remaining meat. Cut meat into 1/2-inch chunks, leaving the tails whole.

Thinly slice the cucumber, leaving the skin on. Peel and de-pit the avocado and cut into thin half-moon slices.

In a small bowl, whisk together extra virgin olive oil, fresh lemon juice, chopped parsley and salt and black pepper. Let the dressing sit for 30 minutes and whisk before serving.

Place cucumber slices in circle in the middle of your plate. Add an inner circle of avocado slices and place lobster on top and topping off with the tails on top.

Drizzle lemon vinaigrette on top. Finish it off with the balsamic glaze drizzled on top.

Orecchiette with Sausage and Spinach

Ingredients
2 tablespoon extra virgin olive oil
1 pound sweet Italian sausage, cut into ½-inch slices (or substitute with turkey sausage)
1 large onion, chopped
2 large garlic cloves, chopped
1 cup low-sodium vegetable broth
10 ounces spinach, coarsely chopped
Pinch red pepper flakes
Sea salt & freshly ground pepper to taste
1 pound Orecchiette
½ cup grated Parmesan

Directions

Sauté garlic and onion for two to three minutes in olive oil, until lightly browned. Add sausage and cook for another five to seven minutes, until no longer pink. Add spinach and vegetable broth and let wilt. Season with salt, pepper and red pepper flakes. Bring a large pot of salted water to a rolling boil, and cook Orecchiette until al dente. Drain pasta and add into pan. Simmer for another 2 minutes. Serve with grated Parmesan on top.

Grilled Angus Sirloin Steak

Ingredients
4 (10 oz) Top Sirloin Steaks
Extra virgin olive oil
2 tablespoons minced garlic
Sea salt & freshly ground pepper to taste

Barolo Reduction Sauce

Ingredients
1 bottle Barolo
1/2 cup shallots, chopped
1 tablespoon extra virgin olive oil
Thyme sprig
Sea salt & freshly ground pepper to taste

Directions
For the steak, season both sides with extra virgin olive oil, garlic, sea salt and pepper until evenly coated. Place steaks on the grill and cook for 8-15 minutes, over high heat depending upon thickness and desired doneness.

For the Barolo reduction sauce heat the oil in a saucepan. Add the shallots and thyme and sauté over high heat for three to four minutes, continuously stirring. Add the wine and reduce for 45 minutes, until consistency thickens. Strain the sauce and drizzle over the steak.

Pecan Pie

Ingredients
2 eggs
1 cup sugar
1/4 cup water
1 tablespoon honey
2 tablespoons flour
1 teaspoon sea salt
1 teaspoon vanilla
1 1/4 cups pecans, coarsely chopped
1/2 cup whole pecans

Directions
Preheat oven to 375 degrees. Lightly beat two eggs and add water, sugar, honey and vanilla. In a separate bowl, mix flour and sea salt together. Slowly add wet mixture into dry mixture and continuously stir. Add chopped pecans into mixture and pour into 9-inch pie shell. Place remaining whole pecans on top and bake for 45-50 minutes until filling is set.

Nautical

Ship Ahoy! Indulge in this menu incorporating dishes from the earth, land and sea. Have your guests enter by walking the plank into their voyage on the seas (simple bridges can be rented at any party prop store). Cover your deck with blue and white linens, adding red accent pieces and anchors throughout. Incorporating simple chalkboard signs saying 'Catch of the Day' will add a nice touch as well. Don't forget to include a photo station, complete with a life preserver and captain hats to commemorate your guests' voyage. Smooth sailing, mates!

Menu

Creole Seared Shrimp Salad
Creole-seasoned shrimp, baby mixed greens

Chicken Satay with Peanut Coconut Sauce
Ginger, cilantro

Monte Cristo
Honey mustard, provolone, Mortadella

Roasted Corn, Wild Mushroom and Spinach Risotto
Chanterelle, oyster and stemmed shiitake

Greek Yogurt Fruit Popsicles
Peaches, lemon, mint

Creole-Seared Shrimp Salad

Creole Seasoning
2 tablespoons paprika
1 tablespoon sea salt
2 tablespoons garlic, minced
1 tablespoon black pepper
1 tablespoon onion powder
1 tablespoon cayenne pepper
1 tablespoon dried oregano
1 tablespoon dried thyme

Dressing Ingredients
1 egg
1 lemon, juiced
1/4 cup onions, chopped
1/4 cup green onions, chopped
1/4 cup celery, chopped
1 tablespoon prepared horseradish
3 tablespoons whole grain mustard
3 tablespoons ketchup
3 tablespoons chopped parsley
Pinch of cayenne pepper
1 cup extra virgin olive oil

4 dozen medium shrimp, peeled and deveined
10 cups assorted summer baby greens
Sea salt & freshly ground pepper to taste

Directions
For the dressing combine egg, lemon juice, onion, green onion, celery, horseradish, mustard, ketchup and parsley in a food processor until smooth. Season with sea salt, pepper and cayenne pepper. Slowly add the oil, constantly whisking, a little at a time, until thick.

For the shrimp, mix all creole ingredients together. Generously coat the shrimp with the creole seasoning and sear the shrimp in a pan over high heat, until just pink.

Toss the lettuce with half of the dressing. Season with sea salt and pepper as needed. Mound the greens in the center of each serving plate. Place shrimp around each mound of greens.

Chicken Satay with Peanut Coconut Sauce

Ingredients
1/2 cup creamy peanut butter
1 cup coconut milk
2 tablespoons fresh lime juice
2 tablespoons soy sauce (low sodium)
1 1/2 teaspoons dark brown sugar
1 teaspoon ground ginger
2 medium sized garlic cloves, chopped
1 3/4 pounds thinly sliced chicken cutlets (organic preferred)
2 tablespoons fresh cilantro, chopped
30 skewers (optional)

Directions
In a large bowl, whisk peanut butter, coconut milk, lime juice, soy sauce, brown sugar, ginger, and garlic. Remove ¾ cup sauce to small bowl and refrigerate for dipping.

Cut chicken cutlets across grain into long strips, about ¾-inch thick. Add chicken strips to large bowl with remaining peanut coconut dipping sauce. Thoroughly coat chicken. Cover and marinate chicken in refrigerator for at least 1 hour.

Bring reserved ¾ cup peanut-coconut dipping sauce to room temperature. Set oven rack four inches from broiler. Heat broiler to medium-high. Thread chicken strip onto each presoaked skewer (optional to use skewers). Arrange chicken in a single layer on prepared rack. You can also grill the chicken skewers.

Broil chicken until browned and cooked through, about 7-10 minutes. Arrange skewers on platter and serve with dipping sauce. Sprinkle chopped cilantro on top.

Monte Cristo

Ingredients
1/4 cup honey mustard
8 slices sourdough bread
4 ounces provolone cheese, sliced
1 cup arugula
1/2 pound Mortadella, sliced
1/2 cup 1% milk
4 large egg whites
2 teaspoons powdered sugar
1 tablespoon vegetable oil
1/2 cup blackberry preserves

Directions
Spread honey mustard over each bread slice. Place two slices of cheese over each of four bread slices. Distribute Mortadella slices over cheese and add fresh arugula to each piece. Top with remaining bread slices. In a shallow bowl, whisk milk and egg whites. Dip both sides of each sandwich into milk mixture, removing any excess milk.

Heat a large nonstick skillet coated with vegetable oil over high heat. Cook sandwiches, until lightly browned and the cheese has melted, about four minutes per slice. Sprinkle sandwiches with confectioners' sugar and top with blackberry preserves.

Roasted Corn, Wild Mushroom and Spinach Risotto

Ingredients
1 pound sweet corn kernels
4 tablespoons extra virgin olive oil
2 cups assorted wild mushrooms (chanterelle, oyster and shiitake) thinly sliced
2 tablespoons chopped fresh thyme
3 cups low-sodium vegetable stock
1 1/4 cups finely chopped onion
1 1/2 cups Arborio rice
1/4 cup dry white wine
2 cups steamed baby spinach
1/2 cup freshly grated Parmesan cheese
1 tablespoon unsalted butter
2 tablespoons chopped chives
1 tablespoon minced garlic

Directions
Preheat oven to 400 degrees. Place corn on baking sheet. Brush with oil. Roast corn until tender and brown in spots, turning occasionally, about 40 minutes. Remove corn from oven, cool and cut off kernels off. You can also use frozen corn.

Toss mushrooms with chopped thyme and 1 tablespoon olive oil on large baking sheet. Sprinkle with sea salt and pepper. Roast mushrooms until tender and golden. About 12-15 minutes at 375 degrees. Combine 2 cups corn and ½ cup vegetable stock in a food processor. Blend until almost smooth. Set corn puree aside.

Heat 2 tablespoons olive oil in a large saucepan over medium heat and sauté garlic and onions. Add rice and continuously stir for three minutes. Add wine and stir until liquid is absorbed, about two minutes. Add 1 cup stock. Simmer until liquid is absorbed, stirring often. Combine additional stock ½ cup at a time until rice is tender, but slightly firm in the center and mixture is creamy. Simmer until stock is absorbed before each addition and stirring often, about 25 minutes.

Mix corn puree, reserved corn kernels, half of mushrooms, spinach, Parmesan cheese and butter into risotto. Stir in 1/3 cup stock to moisten if necessary. Continue cooking until rice is tender. Season to taste with sea salt and pepper. Remove from heat. Spoon risotto into soup bowls. Top with remaining mushrooms. Sprinkle with chives and thinly sliced Parmesan cheese.

Greek Yogurt Fruit Popsicles

Ingredients
2 cups peaches, peeled and sliced
1/2 cup sugar
Juice of 1 lemon
1 teaspoon mint, chopped
4 cups Greek yogurt

Directions
Blend together fruit, sugar and lemon juice. Mix in mint. Combine fruit puree and yogurt, and pour into popsicle mold. Freeze until the popsicles are firm.

California Dreamin'

Surf's up! I'm a California girl at heart and these are some of my favorite dishes to enjoy during the summer. Feel the warmth of the sun by using surfboards as tabletops. Bright beach towel-inspired linens will add the extra pop, while accenting with beach pails. If dining al fresco, incorporate beach chairs into a sandpit so guests can bury their toes in the sand. Beach Boys'-style music will transport your guest to a true California Dreamin' experience.

Menu

Melted Brie with Fruits
Apple, pear, raisins, pecans

Gazpacho with Jumbo Lump Crabmeat
Plum tomatoes, watermelon, cucumber, cantaloupe, lime juice

Coda di Rospo Livornese, (Pan-Seared Monkfish)
Spicy tomato sauce, kalamata olives

Spinach Spaghetti with Sun-Dried Tomatoes
Sun-dried tomatoes, toasted pine nuts, garlic and olive oil

Grilled Pineapple
Cinnamon, brown sugar

Melted Brie with Fruits

Ingredients
1 wheel of Brie
1 apple, peeled and diced
1 pear, peeled and diced
1 cup raisins
1/2 cup pecans, chopped
2 tablespoon honey
1 lemon juiced
1 grapefruit, juiced

Directions
Marinate apple and pear in lemon and grapefruit juice for at least two hours in the refrigerator.

Cut Brie in half, horizontally. Put the first round in a round baking dish. Mix fruit together with raisins and pecans. Top the first brie round with half of the fruit mixture and 1 tablespoon honey. Put the second round on top of the fruit. Put the rest of the fruit mixture and honey on top. Bake uncovered at 350 degrees until cheese is melted and warm. About 30 minutes. Serve with crackers or toasted baguette slices.

Gazpacho with Jumbo Lump Crabmeat

Ingredients
6 peeled plum tomatoes, chopped
1 cup seedless watermelon, chopped
1/2 cup cantaloupe, chopped
2 cucumbers seeded, peeled and chopped
1/2 cup celery chopped
2 cups yellow, green and red pepper, combined and chopped
1/4 cup red onion, diced
1 jalapeño, chopped
1/2 cup cilantro, chopped
1/4 cup basil, chopped
1 fresh lime squeezed
4 cups tomato juice
1 tablespoon red wine vinegar
1 tablespoon Worcestershire sauce
1 teaspoon Tabasco
1 cup extra-virgin olive oil
Sea salt & freshly ground pepper to taste

Toppings
1 pound jumbo lump crabmeat
2 avocados, sliced

Directions
Combine all ingredients together, except the toppings and blend to a chunky consistency using a hand blender. Serve with crabmeat and avocado slices on top. Keep in mind, the longer you let the gazpacho sit, the more flavorful the dish will be.

Monkfish Livornese

Ingredients
4 monkfish fillets (6 oz each)
2 tablespoons extra virgin olive oil
2 garlic cloves, minced
2 eggs
1 cup flour
Sea salt & freshly ground pepper to taste

Livornese Sauce

Ingredients
2 tablespoons extra virgin olive oil
2 small onions, chopped
4 garlic cloves, sliced
29 ounces tomato sauce
6 ounces tomato paste and three cans of water. Use the tomato paste can to fill the water
2 teaspoons thyme leaves
1 cup kalamata olives, pit removed, sliced
1 cup basil leaves, chopped
1 tablespoon capers
1/4 cup chopped parsley
1/4 teaspoon red pepper flakes
Sea salt & freshly ground pepper to taste

Directions
Season each monkfish fillet with sea salt, pepper and minced garlic. Beat eggs and dip fish fillet in eggs and lightly dust with flour. Heat olive oil in a large skillet and add monkfish. Cook four to five minutes on each side, until golden brown. Keep warm.

For the sauce, heat the olive oil in a large sauce pan and sauté onions and garlic for about three to five minutes. Add tomato sauce and paste, thyme, olives, capers and red pepper flakes. Add basil and parsley and simmer for 45 minutes. Use sea salt and pepper to liking.

Spoon tomato sauce on top of monkfish.

Spinach Spaghetti with Sun-Dried Tomatoes

Ingredients
1 pound spinach spaghetti
1 cup sun-dried tomatoes
2 tablespoons pine nuts
1 tablespoon extra virgin olive oil
1/2 cup low sodium vegetable stock
1/4 teaspoon crushed red pepper flakes
2 minced garlic cloves
1/2 cup grated Parmesan cheese
2 tablespoons flat leaf Italian Parsley, chopped

Directions
Place the pine nuts in a skillet over medium heat, and continuously stir until lightly toasted. Add olive oil and sauté garlic with red pepper flakes. Pour vegetable stock in the pan, and add sun-dried tomatoes. Continue cooking two to three minutes. Season with sea salt and freshly ground pepper. Simmer on low for 15 minutes.

In a large pot, bring salted water to a boil. Place spinach spaghetti in the pot and cook until al dente, (about 12 minutes) and drain. Add cooked pasta into saucepan and gently stir together. Mix in grated cheese. Add chopped parsley on top before serving.

Grilled Pineapple

Ingredients
1 whole pineapple, peeled, cored and sliced into ½ inch chunks
1/2 cup brown sugar
1 teaspoon ground cinnamon
1/2 cup vodka
1 lemon juiced
1 orange juiced

Directions
Combine all ingredients together and let pineapple slices macerate overnight. The longer the pineapple sits, the more intense the flavor will be.

Heat a grill to medium-high heat and grill each slice for three to five minutes per side.

Summertime Favorites

From backyard BBQ's to rooftop soiree's and beach bon fires, summer to me has always been about soaking up the sun and enjoying the outdoors. Clean, fresh and flavorful are how I like to describe summertime meals. Enjoy this collection of additional recipes to enjoy during Summer.

Asparagus Oreganata
Bread crumbs, Parmesan, parsley

Shrimp Scampi
Jumbo shrimp, lemon juice, garlic

Prosciutto and Melon
Blood orange, cantaloupe

Chicken Picatta
White wine, capers, lemon

Asparagus Oreganata

Ingredients
1 pound fresh asparagus, trimmed
2 cups Italian seasoned bread crumbs
1/2 cup freshly grated Parmesan cheese
2 tablespoons extra virgin olive oil
2 garlic cloves, minced
1 tablespoon parsley chopped
Sea salt & freshly ground pepper to taste

Directions
Mix together bread crumbs, sea salt, pepper, garlic, parsley and olive oil. Drizzle over asparagus and let sit for 15-20 minutes. Bake at 375 degrees for 20-25 minutes, until tender.

Shrimp Scampi

Ingredients
2 tablespoons minced garlic
2 pounds jumbo shrimp, deveined
1 teaspoon lemon pepper
2 tablespoons extra virgin olive oil
1/2 cup white wine
1/2 cup low-sodium vegetable stock
1/4 cup freshly squeezed lemon juice
1 tablespoon chopped parsley
1 teaspoon freshly ground black pepper
1/2 teaspoon sea salt

Directions
In a large skillet, heat olive oil and sauté garlic. Add wine, stock, lemon juice, parsley and black pepper and bring it to a simmer until sauce is reduced by half. Toss the shrimp with lemon pepper, salt and pepper. Add to the sauce and cook for two to three minutes or until the shrimp turns pink.

Prosciutto and Melon

Ingredients
1 cantaloupe, seeded and cut into wedges, removed from skin
2/3 pound prosciutto di Parma, thinly sliced
2 blood oranges, juiced

Let cantaloupe slices macerate in blood orange juice for two hours in the refrigerator. Wrap each piece of cantaloupe with a slice of prosciutto.

Chicken Piccata

Ingredients
4 skinless, boneless chicken breasts, pounded thin
1/2 cup flour
1 teaspoon paprika
1 tablespoon butter
2 tablespoons extra virgin olive oil
1/4 cup dry white wine
1/2 cup chicken stock
1/4 cup capers, drained
2 garlic cloves, sliced
1 tablespoon shallot, minced
1 tablespoon parsley, chopped
1/2 lemon, juiced

Directions
Season chicken with sea salt, pepper and paprika. Dredge chicken in flour and remove excess.

In a skillet, heat oil and butter and cook chicken for three to four minutes per side. Add another tablespoon of olive oil and butter if needed for the remaining chicken. Once chicken is cooked remove from pan.

In the same pan, sauté garlic and shallot. Add white wine, chicken stock, lemon juice, capers, parsley, sea salt, pepper and reduced for 10 minutes. Return chicken to the pan for two to three minutes, coating in sauce. Transfer to serving plate and pour sauce on top. Sprinkle freshly chopped parsley.

Chapter 4

Harvesting
September | October | November

Fall is my favorite season. I'll never forget walking through Central Park for the first time, in awe of the beautiful changing colors of the leaves. It signifies summer's end and the start to a brisk holiday season, with comforting, flavors and soothing colors. Fall back, and enjoy nature's beauty.

Autumn Produce Guide

Acorn Squash
Arugula
Belgian Endive
Broccoli
Brussels Sprouts
Butter (Bibb) Lettuce
Buttercup Squash
Butternut Squash
Cauliflower
Daikon Radish

Endive
Hot Peppers
Jerusalem Artichoke
Jicama
Kale
Kohlrabi
Pumpkin
Radicchio
Sweet Potatoes
Swiss Chard
Winter Squash

Asian Pears
Cape Gooseberries
Cranberries
Grapes
Huckleberries

Kumquats
Passion Fruit
Pears
Pomegranate
Quince

Labor Day

Labor Day always signifies that summer is coming to an end. This menu is a great blend final summer tastes while introducing autumn flavors. Simplify your theme with the classic "white party". This is always a simple and classic soiree where guests can be your décor!

Encourage white attire only by all attendees. Incorporate the flow of white sheer curtains to blow in the end of summer breeze. All white décor is easy and fun to do... get creative by accenting your space with oversized white props such as lounge furniture, oversized frames, all white ceramic animals...these make for an eclectic photo backdrop for guests to remember.

Menu

Sollenne Family Rice Balls
Arborio rice, peas, mozzarella, Pecorino Romano

Panzanella (Sicillian Bread Salad)
Beefsteak tomatoes, cucumber, onion, capers

Braised Quail
Stuffed with turkey, wrapped in pancetta, grilled Polenta, balsamic reduction

Bananas Foster
Rum, cinnamon, sugar

Sollenne Family Rice Balls

Ingredients
3 cups Arborio rice
2 cups grated Pecorino Romano cheese
2 cups mozzarella cheese, shredded
2 cups water
1 tablespoon extra virgin olive oil
1/2 cup onion, chopped
1 clove garlic, chopped
1 pound ground beef
1 tablespoon fresh parsley, chopped
1 (6 oz) tomato paste
1 cup frozen peas
2 tablespoons unsalted butter
6 eggs, slightly beaten
2 cups plain bread crumbs (panko)
Vegetable oil for frying

Directions
Sauté chopped garlic in 1 tablespoon olive oil. Add the onions and then ground beef and brown on medium heat. Add 1 tablespoon chopped parsley, tomato paste, 1 cup Pecorino cheese grated, 1 cup peas and 1 cup mozzarella cheese. Cook about 15 minutes.

Boil water, and cook rice. When rice is done stir in butter. Add 1 cup of grated Pecorino, 1 cup of shredded mozzarella cheese and mix well together. Season with sea salt and pepper. Cool rice mixture. Once cooled, scoop out rice and form into a ball. Take your thumb and form a thumbprint in the middle of the ball. Fill with meat mixture and then reform into an enclosed ball.

In a separate bowl, beat eggs, and roll rice balls into the eggs, then panko bread crumbs. Heat vegetable oil and lightly fry rice balls on each side for 3-4 minutes. Remove from oil and poke with a tooth pick. Finish in the oven at 400 degrees for two to three minutes, until outside is nice and crispy. Pair with Nonna Dina's Sauce for dipping (pg.54).

Panzanella (Sicillian Bread Salad)

Ingredients
1 loaf of day-old (or two-day old!) crusty bread (I love using seven-grain Italian bread, but any baguette or ciabatta will work well.)
1 cucumber, seeded and chopped
2 beefsteak tomatoes, chopped
1/2 sweet onion, thinly sliced
2 garlic cloves, chopped
1/2 cup extra virgin olive oil
1/4 cup white wine vinegar
1/2 cup cubed fresh mozzarella cheese
1 tablespoon chopped basil
1 tablespoon capers, drained
1 cup green olives, halved
Sea salt & freshly ground pepper to taste
Dash of oregano

Directions
Cut bread into 1/2" cubes. Add cucumber, tomatoes, onion, capers and olives. Mix together garlic, olive oil, vinegar, oregano and season with sea salt and pepper. Mix well. Add chopped basil and cubes of fresh mozzarella cheese to the salad. Pour dressing over ingredients and gently toss together.

Braised Quail

Ingredients
4 boneless quail
4 ounces ground turkey
8 slices of pancetta
8 sage leaves
1 tablespoon extra virgin olive oil
1 tablespoon chopped parsley
2 garlic cloves, chopped
1 tablespoon sweet onions, chopped
Sea salt & freshly ground pepper to taste
4 toothpicks

Grilled Polenta
Ingredients
2 cups yellow cornmeal
6 cups water
1 teaspoon sea salt
1/2 cup Parmesan cheese
1 tablespoon butter

Reduction Sauce
Ingredients
1 cup balsamic
1/2 cup grenadine
1 teaspoon honey

Directions
In a bowl, mix ground turkey with parsley, garlic, onions and a dash of sea salt and pepper. Stuff ground turkey into the quail, place sage leaves on the outside of the skin. Wrap pancetta slices around the quail and secure with a toothpick. Continue to do this for the remaining pieces.

Heat 1 tablespoon extra virgin olive oil and braise quail for two to three minutes, turning once. Finish in the oven at 400 degrees for seven to eight minutes, or until pancetta becomes crispy.

Gently whisk polenta in salted boiling water, then reduce to a simmer and cook for 15 minutes. Stir in butter and Parmesan cheese until melted. Spread polenta mixture onto a baking sheet and refrigerate for at least two hours, or until hardened. With a circle mold (or shape of preference) cut out polenta. Over medium heat, place polenta on grill for two minutes each side, until grill marks appear.

Finish with a balsamic grenadine reduction. Reduce 1 cup balsamic vinegar, 1/2 cup grenadine and honey into a small pot and simmer for 25-30 minutes, until consistency thickens. Place polenta in the center of a dish with the braised quail on top and drizzle the reduction sauce over.

Bananas Foster

Ingredients
2 tablespoons unsalted butter
1 cup brown sugar
1 teaspoon cinnamon
1/4 cup banana liqueur
4 bananas, cut in half lengthwise and then in half crosswise
1/4 cup dark rum
Vanilla bean ice cream

Directions
Combine butter, sugar and cinnamon in a skillet over low heat and stir until sugar dissolves. Watch heat and stir almost constantly to prevent mixture from burning.

Add banana liqueur. Add bananas and cook until they soften and start to brown. Next, add rum and tip pan slightly so the flames ignite the rum. (This is known as flambéing.) After flames subside, place four pieces of banana over vanilla ice cream and spoon some of the sauce over them. Simple and delicious.

Colors of the Wind

Welcome fall! Wrap yourself in a warm blanket of autumn colors by using deep oranges, purples, and magentas. The colors and tastes of this menu are a nice balance to welcome the season. Play with large, ornate serving dishes in jewel tones to accent your fall table-scapes. Incorporate large, candelabras to enhance the drama of this season. Encourage your guests to come in cocktail attire to exaggerate the colors of the wind...

Menu

French Onion Soup
Thyme, sweet onions

Port-Soaked and Stuffed Figs
Goat cheese, chives, toasted walnuts

Warm Seasonal Vegetable Salad
Beets, brussels sprouts, baby carrots, turnips, mushrooms, ricotta

Braised Beef Short Ribs
Chianti reduction, parsley mashed potatoes

Pumpkin Bread
Nutmeg, cinnamon, pure pumpkin

French Onion Soup

Ingredients
10 medium yellow onions, halved, peeled and thinly sliced
1/2 cup water
2 tablespoons extra virgin olive oil
1/2 tablespoon sugar
1/4 teaspoon dried thyme
3 (14.5 oz) cans or 43.5 ounces chicken broth (reduced sodium)
3/4 cup dry red wine
2 teaspoons sea salt
1 teaspoon freshly ground pepper to taste

Cheese Toast
4 multigrain bread slices
4 ounces sliced Swiss cheese

Directions
Preheat oven to 450 degrees. In a large roasting pan, toss together onions, oil, sugar, thyme, 2 teaspoons sea salt, 1 teaspoon pepper and water. Cover tightly with foil, cook until steamed, about 30 minutes. Uncover and continue cooking while stirring occasionally, until onions are golden brown and caramelized, about one hour.

Transfer onion mixture to a large saucepan (reserve roasting pan), stir in broth and bring to a boil, reduce heat to a simmer for two hours.

Meanwhile, deglaze the roasting pan with red wine. Place the pan over medium heat and add wine. Scrape the bottom of the pan with a wooden spoon or scraper to loosen any browned bits. Simmer until reduced and syrupy, about two minutes. Pour liquid and browned bits into soup. Season with additional sea salt and pepper. (If freezing some to save, let cool completely before transferring to airtight containers, leaving one inch at top)

Place bread on a single layer with cheese on top and broil until toasted and cheese is melted. To serve, divide soup among bowls, garnish each with two triangles of cheese toast.

Port Soaked and Stuffed Figs

Ingredients
12 dried figs, cut in half
1/2 cup port wine
1 teaspoon whole fennel seeds
1/4 teaspoon ground black pepper
1/4 pound goat cheese
1 tablespoon chopped chives
2 tablespoons chopped walnuts

Directions
In a one-quart saucepan, combine the figs, port, fennel seeds and black pepper and bring to a boil. Lower the heat to a simmer, and cover with a lid. Let the figs plump in the port for 15 minutes. Remove the figs from the saucepan, and lay them out on a tray to cool completely.

Thoroughly blend together goat cheese and chives until smooth. Mix in the walnuts.

Place a small dollop of the cheese mixture in the center of each fig, refrigerate for 15 minutes to firm the cheese. Serve cold.

Warm Seasonal Vegetable Salad

Ingredients
12 baby beets
12 brussels sprouts
12 round baby carrots
12 turnips
2 cups mixed mushrooms
2 tablespoons extra virgin olive oil
2 garlic cloves sliced
8 slices of reduced fat ricotta cheese
4 tablespoons balsamic dressing

Directions
Cut all vegetables in half. Boil baby beets for 35 minutes. In one pot, add brussels sprouts, carrots and turnips. Boil together for 7-10 minutes. Heat olive oil over medium heat and sauté garlic. Add mushrooms, and cook for two to three minutes until lightly browned.

Add all cooked vegetables to an oven safe sauté pan and continue cooking for five to seven minutes. Transfer to a preheated 425 degree oven and cook for 20 minutes. Remove vegetables and serve with a balsamic vinaigrette dressing. Season with freshly ground pepper and sea salt. Garnish with slices of reduced fat ricotta cheese. Serve warm and enjoy this nutritious salad!

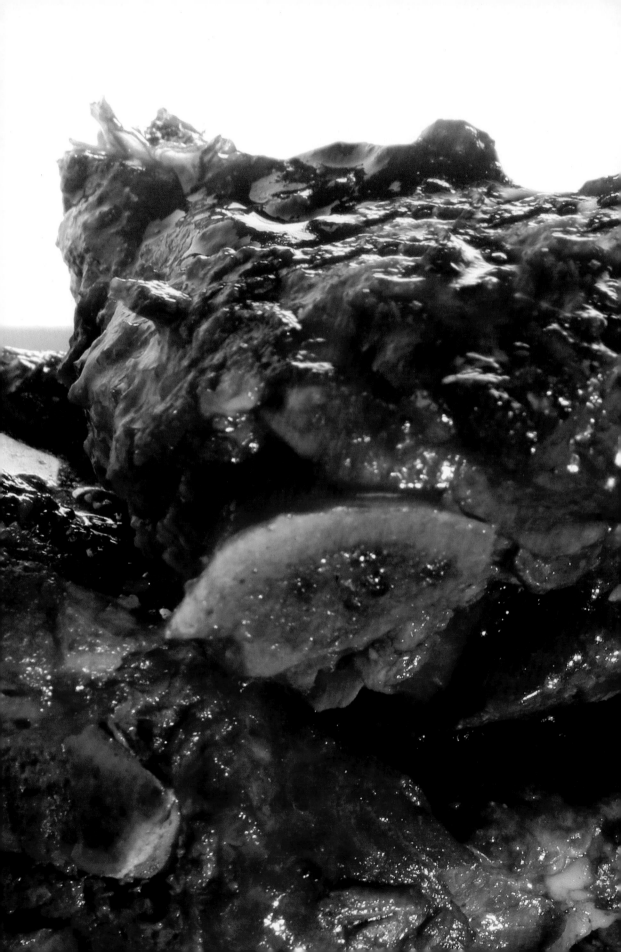

Braised Beef Short Ribs

Ingredients
5 pounds (3-inch thick cut) beef short ribs
1 bunch fresh rosemary, chopped
2 (750-ml) bottles Chianti Classico
1/2 cup extra virgin olive oil, for searing ribs
1 cup yellow onion, diced
1 cup carrots, peeled and diced
2 cups celery, diced
3 cloves garlic, minced
4 quarts beef stock
1 tablespoon honey
1 tablespoon ketchup
1 bay leaf
Sea salt & freshly ground pepper to taste

Directions
Season the ribs with rosemary, sea salt and pepper. Heat a layer of olive oil in a large cast iron pan over medium-high heat. Sear ribs on all sides until well browned. Place browned ribs into a braising or deep roasting pan. Brown onion, carrots, celery, and garlic in the same cast iron pan, adding more oil as needed. Scatter browned vegetables over the ribs. Pour wine, stock, honey and ketchup over the ribs and add bay leaves.

Preheat oven to 375 degrees. Cover the pan with foil and place in the oven for four hours. Transfer from the oven and allow the ribs to rest for one hour before removing the bones. Skim any fat from the sauce. Remove vegetables from the pan and set aside. While ribs are resting, strain sauce into a saucepot and reduce for 45 minutes to one hour, until consistency thickens. Pour reduced sauce over ribs and vegetables and serve. (Instead of roasting in the oven, you can also use a slow cooker)

To add a nice infused flavor to your mashed potatoes, puree fresh flat leaf parsley, about ¾ cup with 3 tablespoons olive oil. Add 1 tablespoon puree into 1 pound mashed potatoes, or until color and taste is to your liking.

Pumpkin Bread

Ingredients
3 1/2 cups all-purpose flour
2 teaspoons baking soda
2 teaspoons sea salt
1 teaspoon baking powder
1 teaspoon ground nutmeg
1 teaspoon ground allspice
1 teaspoon ground cinnamon
1/2 teaspoon ground cloves
3 cups sugar
1 cup canola oil
4 eggs, beaten
2 cups pumpkin
2/3 cup water
1/2 cup candied pecans, loosely chopped

Directions
Preheat oven to 350 degrees. Grease two loaf pans. In a medium-mixing bowl, combine flour, baking soda, sea salt, baking powder, nutmeg, allspice, cinnamon and cloves.

In a large bowl with an electric mixer, blend sugar, oil, and eggs. Stir in pumpkin. Slowly blend the flour mixture into pumpkin mixture. While blending the mixture add water incrementally. Pour the batter into two prepared loaf pans. Sprinkle chopped pecans on top.
Bake for 90 minutes. Let cool for 10 minutes before removing from the oven.

ROCK-TOBERFEST

Why not change up the feel of October by welcoming the coolness of the month, setting the tone for a Rock-toberfest with an all-out clam bake? Dig out your favorite types of music, whether it be classic rock or a rock opera, and have fun with this theme. Serving up your favorite Oktoberfest food, add to the feel by playing various types of music and genres... incorporate mini instruments as your focal points around the space, perhaps even a friendly competition of air guitar will be welcomed. Rock on!

Menu

Clam Bake
Sweet potatoes, corn, clams, lobster, lemon juice

Spicy Pumpkin Soup
Cumin, garbanzo beans, corn, pure pumpkin

Fettuccine with Roasted Butternut Squash
Eggplant and oyster mushrooms

Veal Scallopini
Paprika, nutmeg, garlic cloves

Bourbon Balls
Candied pecans, chocolate

Clam Bake

Ingredients
1 1/2 pounds seaweed
6 small sweet potatoes or yams, scrubbed
6 ears corn, shucked (husks reserved)
1 teaspoon ground black pepper
1 teaspoon sea salt (if not using seaweed)
4 sprigs fresh thyme
4 live lobsters (about 1 pound each)
3 pounds littleneck clams
2 pounds mussels, cleaned and debearded
3 cups dry white wine
1 cup sweet onion, sliced
1/2 cup unsalted butter
1/4 cup extra virgin olive oil
2 tablespoons fresh lemon juice
Lemon wedges

Directions
Combine the butter and lemon juice in a small bowl, set aside. Preheat the grill to high heat. Place metal steamer rack in bottom of a 16-quart pot at least 10 inches in diameter. If using seaweed, place half of it on and under the steamer rack. Add sweet potatoes and onions. Stand corn along edges of pot, stem-end down. Sprinkle with pepper and thyme.

Add the lobsters. Place the clams and mussels, tied loosely in cheesecloth, over the lobsters. Pour wine over. Place a layer of seaweed and/or corn husks on the top and cover with lid.

Place the pot on fire grate over a white-hot fire (adding more briquettes first if necessary) or on a stove over high heat. Cook until a strong gush of steam escapes (about 12 minutes on the stove, about 35 minutes on the grill). Reduce the stove heat to medium-high (leave the outdoor fire as is) and start timing. Steam-cook for about 15 minutes or until the potatoes are tender and the lobsters are bright red. Discard seaweed or corn husks. Arrange the lobsters and other ingredients on a large serving platter. Pour remaining sauce over the seafood and serve with lemon butter and lemon wedges.

Spicy Pumpkin Soup

Ingredients
1 tablespoon canola oil
1 tablespoon minced garlic
1 teaspoon cumin
8 ounces garbanzo beans
1 cup sweet corn kernels
15 ounces solid pack pumpkin
4 cups chicken broth
1 cup Crème fraiche
1 cup cheddar cheese, grated

Directions
Sauté the garlic and cumin in oil for one minute. Add the chicken broth and stir until blended. Add garbanzo beans, corn and pumpkin. Stir in crème fraiche and simmer for 45 minutes. Serve with a dollop of crème fraiche and grated Cheddar cheese on top.

Fettuccine with Roasted Butternut Squash, Eggplant and Oyster Mushrooms

Ingredients
2 cups butternut squash, diced into ½ inch-thick cubes
2 cups eggplant, diced into ½ inch-thick cubes
1 cup sliced oyster mushrooms
1/4 cup extra virgin olive oil
1/2 cup white wine
2 chopped garlic cloves
1 pound fettuccine
Sea salt & freshly ground pepper to taste
½ cup Parmesan cheese
3 tablespoons Italian flat leaf Parsley, chopped

Directions
Sauté butternut squash and eggplant cubes in olive oil and garlic until softened. Add oyster mushroom slices, along with white wine, 1 tablespoon parsley, sea salt and pepper to taste. Bring a large pot of salted water to a boil, and cook fettuccine until al dente. Strain and add cooked pasta into the saucepan and cook an additional two to three minutes. Transfer to serving plate and enjoy! Top with parsley and Parmesan cheese.

Veal Scallopini

Ingredients
2 pounds veal cutlet, thinly sliced
1 1/4 teaspoons sea salt
1 1/2 teaspoons paprika
2 tablespoons extra virgin olive oil
1/3 cup freshly squeezed lemon juice
2 garlic cloves, minced
2 teaspoons prepared mustard
1/2 teaspoon nutmeg
1/3 cup flour
1 large onion, sliced thin
10 ounces chicken broth
1/3 pound fresh mushrooms cleaned and sliced
2 tablespoons butter
12 pimento olives, sliced
1 tablespoon Italian flat leaf Parsley, chopped

Directions
For the sauce heat olive oil and sauté garlic. Combine sea salt, paprika, lemon juice, mustard, butter and nutmeg. Simmer for ten minutes. Place veal flat in baking dish, pour sauce over veal and turn to coat. Let marinate for about 15-20 minutes on each side. Flour each veal side well, and return to skillet to brown with sauce, about 1 minute on each side. Remove veal slices from pan. Add chicken broth and mushrooms. Simmer for ten minutes, then add olives and parsley. Cook and stir five minutes longer until sauce has thickened. Pour sauce over veal and serve.

Bourbon Balls

Ingredients
2 cups finely chopped pecans
1/3 cup bourbon
1/4 cup unsalted butter, softened
1/2 pound powdered sugar
8 ounces bittersweet chocolate, melted

Directions
In a small bowl, soak the pecans in bourbon for at least 30 minutes. In a large bowl, cream together the butter and powdered sugar. Add the pecans and bourbon and stir to combine well. Roll the mixture into small balls and dip balls in melted chocolate. Cool on parchment paper. You can place them in the refrigerator to harden and cool. Roll cooled balls in additional powdered sugar.

Thankful Tummies

Thanksgiving is one of my favorite holidays completely devoted to giving thanks. My fondest memories are cooking in the kitchen with my mom, and setting a beautiful table for our friends and family joining us for the celebration.

Spice up your dinner with a fun theme that all of your guests will remember for a long time. From apple cider to pumpkins, you can create an atmosphere sure to wow! Focus your decorations around celebrating the harvest. Use organic elements such as gourds, Indian corn, a large woven cornucopia, or dried flowers to evoke fall's abundance. Cover your table in burlap and use wooden serving utensils for a rustic feel. Using red, orange, and yellow colors of the changing leaves to give your home a rich autumnal ambiance, so that the room will glow with the warmth of the season and these colors also pop beautifully in flickering candlelight.

Menu

Clam Chowder
Potatoes, pancetta

Tenderloin with Peppercorn Butter
Parsley, ground mustard, peppercorns

Camembert Gratin
Cauliflower, truffle oil

Sollenne Family Meatloaf
Ground meat, green peppers, onion, celery

Sweet Potato Pie
Ginger, brown sugar, lemon juice

Clam Chowder

Ingredients
4 ounces pancetta, diced
1 1/2 cups onion, chopped
1 cup water
2 cups peeled and cubed potatoes
1 1/2 teaspoons sea salt
1 quart half and half
3 tablespoons unsalted butter
10 ounces minced clams
1/2 cup clam juice
Sea salt & freshly ground pepper to taste

Directions
Place diced pancetta in a large stockpot over medium-high heat. Cook until almost crisp, then add onions, and cook five minutes. Stir in water and potatoes, and season with sea salt and pepper. Bring to a boil and simmer uncovered for about one hour or until potatoes are fork tender.

Pour in half and half and add butter. Stir in clams and add calm juice into the soup. Simmer for 25-30 additional minutes stirring constantly.

Tenderloin with Peppercorn Butter

Ingredients
1 (3 ½ - 4 pound) center cut beef tenderloin
2 tablespoons of butter, softened
4 tablespoons extra virgin olive oil
1/2 cup chopped parsley
2 teaspoons freshly ground black pepper
1 teaspoon lemon juice
1 teaspoon ground mustard
1/3 cup crushed peppercorns
2 cloves garlic, minced
1/3 cup red wine

Directions
Trim all of the visible fat off of the tenderloin. Combine butter, olive oil, parsley, black pepper, lemon juice, mustard, garlic and peppercorns. Preheat oven to 425 degrees. Place the tenderloin on a roasting rack and roughly rub peppercorn butter all over. Drizzle red wine over tenderloin. Cook uncovered for 40 minutes. Remove from oven and let sit for 20 minutes before slicing.

Camembert Gratin

Ingredients
2 ounces Camembert cheese with rind, cubed
1 1/2 pounds baking potatoes, peeled and thinly sliced
2 cups finely chopped cauliflower
1/2 yellow onion, thinly sliced
2 tablespoons extra virgin olive oil
1 garlic clove, minced
1 cup heavy cream
1 cup whole milk
1 tablespoon chopped parsley
1 teaspoon white truffle oil
Sea salt & freshly ground pepper to taste

Directions
Preheat oven to 400 degrees. Heat olive oil over medium heat and sauté garlic and onions until tender. Add the cauliflower slices and continue stirring, about five to six minutes.

Add the cream and milk and bring to a simmer. Drizzle truffle oil. Season with sea salt and pepper and add chopped parsley. Add the Camembert cubes and continue stirring until melted. Remove from heat and let cool.

Spread the potatoes and cream mixture into a gratin dish (11" will work well). Bake uncovered at 400 degrees for 25-30 minutes, until golden brown on top.

Sollenne Family Healthy Meatloaf

Ingredients
1 pound ground lean turkey
3/4 cup diced tomatoes
1 cup plain bread, cut into cubes
1/2 cup milk
2 eggs
2 teaspoons Worcestershire
1/2 cup chopped green peppers
1/2 cup chopped onion
1/2 cup chopped celery
1/4 cup ketchup
1 1/2 teaspoons pepper
1 tablespoon chopped parsley
1/2 cup Parmesan cheese, grated

Directions
Whisk together milk and eggs. Soak the bread for 15 minutes. Mix together turkey, tomatoes, green peppers, onions, celery, ketchup, black pepper, and bread squeezed of extra juice, and Worcestershire sauce. Mix in parsley and cheese. Bake at 350 degrees for one hour.

Sweet Potato Pie

Ingredients
3 eggs, beaten
1 cup brown sugar
2/3 cup milk
1/2 teaspoon nutmeg
1 1/4 teaspoons cinnamon
1/2 teaspoon ginger
1/4 cup lemon juice
2 tablespoons unsalted butter, melted
2 cups sweet potato, peeled and cut into 1 inch cubes
9-inch, unbaked pie shell

Directions
Preheat oven to 375 degrees. Combine eggs, brown sugar, milk, nutmeg, cinnamon and ginger. Mix well. Blend in lemon juice and butter. Boil potatoes in a large pot of salted water for 45 minutes, or until fork tender. Add sweet potatoes to pie mixture and whisk to blend together well. Pour mixture into the pie shell and bake for 50 minutes.

Fall Favorites

Fall is a collection of magical memories for me. Growing up, this is when we would turn to baking. So many decedent ingredients and flavors to use and pair together. We always had family and friends visit for the holidays, and there's a magical aroma that fills the house with love when something's baking in the oven. Nothing warms the house more than waking everyone up to the smell of French toast, pancakes and scones! You can't find a better wake-up call than that! Use this collection of recipes to fill your home with pure bliss.

Pasta Piselli
Ditalini, peas, peperoncino

Festive Scones
Currants, sugar, cinnamon

French Toast stuffed with Bananas and Blueberries
Vanilla, banana, blueberry

Lemon Pancakes
Creme fraiche, lemon zest

Monkey Bread
Raisins, walnuts, cinnamon

Pasta Piselli
(Pasta and Peas)

I grew up on very simple, yet flavorful, dishes, which I believe is the best way to cook. Fresh in-season ingredients truly enhance any dish, and my main reminder to everyone is to keep it simple! This is one of my favorite dishes from Nonna.

Ingredients
1 pound Ditalini pasta
1 package frozen peas
2 tablespoons extra virgin olive oil
2 garlic cloves, minced
1 onion, chopped
1/2 cup vegetable broth (Low sodium)
1/2 cup grated Parmesan cheese
1 teaspoon red pepper flakes
1/4 cup reserved pasta water

Directions
In a large sauté pan, heat olive oil and sauté garlic and onion for two to three minutes. Add peas and vegetable broth. Simmer until stock is absorbed about 12-15 minutes. Season with sea salt and pepper and crush red pepper flakes through your palms and add into pan.

In a large pot of boiling salted water, cook pasta for six to seven minutes. Transfer to sauté pan with peas and add in ¼ cup pasta water. Finish cooking until al dente, about three to four minutes longer. Mix in Parmesan cheese and serve.

Festive Scones

Ingredients
1/2 cup currants
Juice of one orange
2 1/2 cups sifted all-purpose flour
3 teaspoons baking powder
1 teaspoon sea salt
1/3 cup sugar
1/2 cup unsalted butter, cut into small cubes
1 egg, beaten
3/4 cup milk
1 teaspoon cinnamon
2 tablespoons sugar

Directions
Preheat oven to 375 degrees. Soak currants in juice of one orange for 20 minutes. In a bowl, sift together flour, baking powder, sea salt and 1/3 cup sugar. Cut in butter until mixture resembles coarse grain. Drain currants, pat dry, and add.

Beat egg until foamy and mix in 1/3 cup milk. Make a well in the center of the flour mixture and pour in beaten egg with milk. Gradually mix together. Add remainder of milk slowly, mixing with a fork until dough clings together. It should be slightly sticky, but not wet.

Turn onto a lightly floured board. Pat dough into one circle about one inch thick. Cut dough into even triangles. Brush triangles lightly with remaining milk and sprinkle cinnamon and sugar on top. Using a spatula, transfer to a buttered cookie sheet. Cook for 15-20 minutes at 375 degrees. Cool on a wire rack.

French Toast stuffed with Bananas and Blueberries

Ingredients
6 tablespoons butter, softened
2 tablespoons sugar
2 tablespoons water
4 large ripe bananas, cut into ½ inch thick rounds
1 cup blueberries
1 loaf of egg bread
2 cups milk
6 large eggs
2 1/2 teaspoon ground cinnamon
1 teaspoon vanilla extract
1/4 cup packed brown sugar
1/4 cup cooking oats
1 cup flour

Directions
Melt 2 tablespoons of butter in a nonstick skillet until melted. Add 2 tablespoons sugar and 2 tablespoons water. Stir until sugar is dissolved. Continue cooking until mixture is foamy then add bananas and blueberries. Cook until tender, stirring occasionally, about five minutes. Transfer to a bowl and cool. Preheat oven to 350 degrees. Cut six slices of bread from the loaf, making each piece 1 ½ inches thick. Cut a slit in one side of the bread almost to the other end and stuff with bananas and blueberries. Do this for the remaining slices.

Whisk milk, eggs, ½ teaspoon cinnamon, vanilla in a large bowl. Blend well. Coat bread thoroughly in the egg mixture on both sides. When bread is well coated, place on a large baking sheet. Mix brown sugar, oats, flour and 2 teaspoons of cinnamon in a bowl. Add ½ stick of butter and rub between your fingers until moist clumps form. Sprinkle topping over each slice of bread. Bake until French toast is golden brown, about 25 minutes on 375 degrees. Serve with maple syrup.

Lemon Pancakes

Ingredients
1/2 cup crème fraiche
1 tablespoon unsalted butter, melted
2 eggs
2 cups flour
1 teaspoon baking powder
2 tablespoons sugar
1/2 cup freshly squeezed lemon juice
1 tablespoon lemon zest
1 tablespoon vegetable oil

Directions
Mix the crème fraiche, melted butter and egg in a bowl and beat well. Add lemon juice and zest, mix well. Combine the flour and sugar, and stir in wet batter, but do not over mix. Preheat a griddle or nonstick pan to medium heat and add vegetable oil. Pour the pancake mixture in pan to desired size and cook 2 -3 minutes until browned on bottom. Flip pancake and brown opposite side. Makes about 15 silver-dollar-sized pancakes.

Monkey Bread

Ingredients
3 (12 oz) packages refrigerated biscuit dough
1 cup sugar
2 teaspoons ground cinnamon
1/2 cup butter
1 cup packed brown sugar
1/2 cup chopped walnuts
1/2 cup raisins

Directions
Preheat oven to 350 degrees. Grease one 10-inch pan. Mix sugar and cinnamon. Cut biscuits into quarters. Coat six to eight biscuit pieces in the sugar and cinnamon mixture. Arrange pieces in the bottom of the prepared pan. Continue until all biscuits are coated and placed in pan. Arrange nuts and raisins in and among the biscuit pieces as you go along.

In a small saucepan, melt the butter with the brown sugar over medium heat. Boil for one minute. Pour over the biscuits. Bake at 350 degrees for 35 minutes. Let bread cool in pan for 8-10 minutes then turn out onto a plate. The bread just pulls apart.

Arrivederci!

Cooking and entertaining for me has always been about bringing people together and creating memorable experiences. I truly hope that my menus and stories have inspired you to entertain with passion and flair!

Visit kristinsollenne.com to learn more about CELLINI aprons and discover great tips and new menu ideas! Follow me @KristinSollenne and lets keep in touch.

Acknowledgments

For my dear friend and colleague, Monica Kline-Kazas, for providing innovative décor tips to enhance my menus. Thank you for always seeing the big picture with me.

For the very talented photographer, Anirays Camino, who captured beautiful photos and truly brought to life the vibrancy and freshness of my cooking.

Author Bio

Celebrity Chef & TV Personality, Kristin Sollenne

Executive Chef / Culinary Director, Certified Nutritionist & Wellness Consultant

As a rising culinary star and Food Network Judge, Chef Kristin Sollenne has been making headlines for her contemporary food philosophy, lightened-up Italian fare, and approachable cooking tips, with regular appearances on WCBS's Morning News and WLNY's "Live from the Couch," as well as a feature on NBC's Today Show, Fox5 Good Day New York, Fox Business and guest judge on NBC's Beat Bobby Flay, and Kitchen Casino. In 2014, she was featured on season ten of Food Network Star as a mentor to finalist Luca Della Casa.

Sollenne, a 2013 honoree of Zagat's Top 30 under 30, has cooked for Taylor Swift, Seth Rogan, Ed Sheeran, and the entire SNL cast. She oversees the three kitchens of the New York City Restaurant Group's (NYCRG) Bocca Di Bacco. "My main philosophy is farm to-table, with a focus on clean ingredients and keeping it simple," the 28-year-old chef says. "I think simple dishes speak a lot louder than over-complicated ones. Simplicity actually enhances the flavors."

Sollenne's other culinary tenets for modernizing Italian cuisine include moderating portion sizes and using nutritious and full-flavored alternative ingredients. She centers most menu items on farm-fresh vegetables and herbs, lean proteins, whole grains, and heart-healthy olive oil, while limiting the amount of butter and cream. "I get asked a lot, 'How can you make healthy Italian food?' she says. "It's all about the choices you make. You can still cook satisfying, great-tasting dishes on the lighter side when you use fresh, in-season products. Or I'll make pasta with whole wheat, or spinach spaghetti, so it's not just all about heavy starches."

The self-taught chef discovered her interest and talent in creating fresh spins on classic Italian dishes while she was growing up in California with her Italian-American family. She honed in on creating wholesome meals without compromising on flavor as she assisted her parents in attaining their weight-loss goals while still enjoying their favorite foods. "Cooking for my parents really ignited that spark for me to move to New York and getting involved in the restaurant industry here."

Sollenne has worked with the NYCRG since 2008, bringing a California farm-to-table mind-set to traditional Southern Italian cuisine. In her role as executive chef and culinary director, she oversees the expanding chain, works with each location's chefs on nutritious cooking techniques, and manages the training program as well as implementing new, innovative menu developments. Prior to helming culinary operations at Bocca Di Bacco, she served as opening chef at NYCRG's Vucciria in the Theater District, which she helped rebrand into another Bocca Di Bacco in summer 2012. When not designing the next reimagined dish or catering and designing exquisite events, the Upper West Side resident enjoys running, dancing, and traveling for food inspiration.